Five
Eminent
Contrarians:

Careers, Perspectives and Investment Tactics

By Steven L. Mintz

FRASER PUBLISHING COM
Burlington, V

Published by Fraser Publishing Company
a division of Fraser Management Associates, Inc.
P.O. Box 494
Burlington, VT 05402

Library of Congress Catalog Card Number: 94-72582

ISBN: 0-87034-115-4

Printed in the United States of America
Cover Design by John McLaughlin
Designed and Produced by PostScript, Inc.

To W.B.M. and H.J.M.,
With love

Table of Contents

Acknowledgements

LIKE ANY LARGE EFFORT, THIS BOOK IS A PRODUCT OF A FAR larger cast than the author alone. I am indebted to Wayne Welch for many valuable suggestions and to Martha Jewett and Jim Childs for initial encouragement and guidance. Thanks are due also to Ed Finn, for easing my transition from a real job into the strange and borderless business of writing a book, and to Al Ehrbar, for sharing his vast knowledge of finance. I am grateful to John McLaughlin, whose wisdom and expertise transcend the book cover he designed and to John Goff and Stuart Flack for encouraging words at difficult turning points.

My supporting cast includes also Jim Fraser, who rescued this book when my own determination to see it through faltered, and Sam Newborn, who did his best to keep it from faltering. I also must thank Tom Tisch for key insights that helped shape my perspective on contrarian investing, and John Jakobson and Ned Whitcraft for putting in needed words with sources who normally shy away from attention, and Al Neill for exceptional hospitality. Needless to say, the five investors I have profiled are not the only eminent contrarians. Others, notably Bob Torray, Charles Wohlstetter, Jim Tisch, Ambassador Shelby Davis and Marc Faber, were of great help to me. My gratitude extends also to the late Bill Gardner, a true friend who taught me to recognize risks worth taking. I could not have written this book, either, without my father's intelligent and gracious input and my mother's mellow outlook on life. My two sons, Ben and Thomas, deserve thanks for letting me work when I sought distraction. But my greatest thanks goes to my wife, Melissa Whitcraft, for her patience and support every inch along a tortuous path.

Introduction

Follow the course opposite to custom
and you will almost always do well.
- Jean Jacques Rousseau

SUCCESSFUL CONTRARIAN INVESTORS SELDOM FIT THE POPULAR mold. They are not high rollers chasing astronomical rewards. Short contrarian careers are built on grandiose schemes and knee-jerk reactions to apparent market behavior. The five contrarians in this book are responsible, cautious, disciplined and, for the most part, risk averse. They stay around for the long term. They know that the way to create wealth, and keep it, is to stay away from the crowd, especially when euphoria or despair prevails.

Confusion about who really is contrarian springs from the difficulty defining contrarian. In their hefty and definitive *Investment Strategy and Portfolio Management*, authors Jerome Cohen, Edward Zinbarg and Arthur Zeikel agreed that there is no precise definition. "Contrary opinion in the stock market is actually an attitude or intellectual process, not a tool of technical analysis... However, the general concept is to go against the crowd. Humphrey Neill, generally considered the father of contrary opinion, put it this way: 'When everyone thinks alike, everyone is likely to be wrong.'"

Evidence corroborating Neill is not hard to find. Just consider a 1992 study of the way investors choose mutual funds. Co-sponsored by Oppenheimer Management and the *Wall*

Street Journal, the study concluded that mutual fund investors really don't know what they are doing. "If you buy and sell with the mutual fund crowd, you are likely to get rotten results," the *Journal* reported. "The trend investors tend to buy high and sell low," Oppenheimer Chairman Jon Fossel told the *Journal*. Investors who followed the herd each time it stampeded for the mutual fund with the strongest results ended up with a meager 20 percent return after five and one-half years. Average funds produced 42 percent. A contrarian strategy, selling what was most popular and buying what was least popular, would have returned nearly twice the average.

Books have been written before on contrarian investing techniques, even though, as Messrs. Cohen, Zinbarg and Zeikel pointed out, contrarian investing is more than just a technique. This book is different. It tackles contrary investing by probing the minds, personalities and careers of investors not burdened by the millstone of prevailing opinion.

The intent is not to be comprehensive, but to present a cross section of the most intelligent and interesting contrarian investors in the context of their times. Their eclectic ranks include Humphrey Neill, the Vermont Ruminator; John Neff, the savvy manager of the $10.5 billion Windsor Fund; Dean LeBaron, a pension fund guru who sold popcorn in New Guinea to prove that opportunities exist at all times in all places; David Babson, who foresaw prosperity after World War II while most investors waited for the depression to resume; and Michael Aronstein, a contemplative investment manager whose vision of capitalism's future draws inspiration from philosophers and poets.

These diverse investors seem to share an inborn sense of supply and demand—or, maybe, demand and supply—that does not get jostled by the crowd. They stand prevailing wisdom on its head to see if it has feet (and in the stock market, it usually does not). As the late Bradbury Thurlow put it in *Rediscovering the Wheel: Contrary Thinking & Investment Strategy*, "Contrary thinking is a deliberate shaking of the mind back and forth, reversing and reaffirming plausible views to separate out the non-essential, much as the gold panner shakes out unwanted pebbles."

In retrospect, what authentic contrarians do is usually obvious. So obvious that lots of investors imagine that they are as contrarian as the next person (paradoxical as that sounds). Given a chance to go back in time, who is not courageous enough to snap up paintings by Henri Matisse when he was a struggling artist? Shrewd judgment is easy to come by after the fact. But cleaning out Matisse's atelier *now* is no more contrarian than buying toothpaste on sale. Investors who think otherwise overlook the withering disapproval that confronted prospective art investors of that day, or else overestimate their ability to disregard it. These investors confuse hindsight and foresight. Matisse's "Woman With a Hat" helps paint the real picture. "It took more than a little courage to buy a masterpiece so jeered at that the artist dared visit the show only once and his wife not at all," Aline B. Saarinen reported in *The Proud Pos-*

sessors. When Ms. Saarinen's book was published in 1958, the masterpiece that went begging at the turn of the century was worth $100,000. Today it is worth far more.

False contrarians abound particularly at turning points, when events or series of events replace what everyone thought was true with, frequently, a more sober assessment. The eighties supplied plenty of examples, most notably the rise and inevitable collapses of oil and real estate prices. Just a few days before the Dow Jones Industrial Average plunged 500 points in October 1987, *Barron's* published an article entitled *Everyone's a Contrarian*. The author, John Schulz, observed that "If there is anything at all to the idea of contrarianism, the true contrarians will be proven right in the end, even if they have to suffer bloody decimation." Schulz assigned the term "pseudo-contrarian" to noisy ranks of investors who carped that fears of a downward correction were overstated. "And quite clearly," Schulz wrote, "today's honest-to-goodness contrarians are those who think the bull market is, and for some time has been, off the wall. No less clearly, they are a minority in the marketplace, which is what true contrarians should be."

All investors require perspective, of course. But it has extra resonance for contrarians, who shun the comfort of the crowd's approval. A unique perspective may be their only company until a turning point vindicates a contrarian strategy. But no one can predict when a trend will exhaust itself.

This much is clear: times are changing. It is not the eighties any more, a decade when the smart way to get rich was to stand in the line that moved fastest. So far, the nineties are proving inscrutable. Contrarians take note. Climates like this are cradles of mass delusion.

Above all, it is worth remembering that contrarian investing is primarily a state of mind. It does not demand vast quantities of research or two years of business school. Then where should someone go to elicit contrary opinions? Listen to the advice that former Fidelity Investments Chairman Edward C. Johnson 2d gave to the fledgling sales force that helped build a mutual fund company that manages $185 billion today.

> All of us have inside of us a part of the crowd. I have always wondered about Humphrey [Neill] and where he gets his dope on what general opinions are. I never have to go outside the confines of my own room. Every one of us has a tuning fork inside of himself that vibrates to a greater or lesser extent along with the crowd. It works so uniformly that when sometimes I talk to salesmen of mutual funds I give them a rule, which is this: That the more it hurts them and the more they have to fight themselves to make a sale, the better it will be for the customer and also for the salesman himself. And that just means going contra to his inborn crowd segment.

Although every investor possesses the capacity to become a contrarian, that won't happen. For one thing, it takes some pain, as Mr. Johnson said. For another, there is a built-in lid on the contrarian population. Genuine contrarians will recognize it by instinct. It is akin to the old riddle that asks how far a dog can run into the woods. The answer is halfway. After that, he's running out.

Montclair, New Jersey
June 1994

Chapter One

*I*NVESTORS WHO WANT TO ESCAPE THE CROWD WILL FIND VALU-*able clues in the personality of **Dean LeBaron**, an investment manager whose idiosyncratic world view reflects a relentless aversion to conventional thinking. His prestigious citation in June 1993 for Distinguished Alumni Achievement, by the Harvard Business School, offered this accolade: "Stellar student of securities, institutional investor extraordinaire, your storied successes as a contrarian are legion and legendary." The peripatetic and outspoken founder and chairman of Batterymarch Financial Management supplies fresh perspectives on any topic, from stocks to quantum physics. In his ever-expanding universe, investor psychology connects seemingly remote worlds. Like a physicist who removes himself one step in order to study light, which cannot be observed directly without disturbing its behavior, LeBaron steps back from the stock market to study other investors. Then he charts a new path.*

Dean LeBaron

Thoughts While Not Shaving

AT THE HEIGHT OF THE SHORT-LIVED COUP AGAINST THE CRUM-bling Soviet government of Mikhail Gorbachev in summer 1991, tanks surrounding the Yeltsin enclave in the Russian White House opened ranks to let a limousine depart. The passenger, Mr. Vitaly Shlikov, deputy chairman of the Committee for Defense and Security of the Soviet Union, was on his way to an important meeting— but not to negotiate the future of the Soviet Union with hard-liners who seized control the day before. He was on his way to a reception aimed at fostering economic ties with private U.S. investors. The host was Dean LeBaron, chairman of Batterymarch Financial Management Corporation and self-appointed tsar of institutional investment in the former Soviet Union.

Two months later, LeBaron is recounting the story for a group of pension executives in New York. This is not the sort of audience that warms quickly to ventures that sound contrarian. No fool, LeBaron concedes that investing in Russia is nothing if it isn't risky. But that is precisely why LeBaron is trying to sell the idea to some of the most conservative investors in America. He conjures up the image of American entrepreneurs more than a century ago, who persuaded the consummately conservative Scottish Investment Board to back railroads across the American frontier. LeBaron wants to do the same, only he is hunting for capital to link the last European frontier to the rest of the world. Excessive caution will smother the opportunity of a lifetime, he warns pension managers. But their appetites for adventure stop with investing in troubled banks.

Playing to skeptical audiences energizes LeBaron; it may even be the aspect of his job that he relishes most. Part securities analyst, part entrepreneur, part evangelist and part missionary, he is the human equivalent of a satellite dish tuned to several frequencies at once. Bounding from one inspiration to another, seldom pausing in between, the restless chairman of Batterymarch Financial Management would love to entertain them all, whether or not anyone else follows.

"The trick of being contrarian is to be early, not just different," LeBaron says. To that end, he exhibits an inexhaustible appetite for exploring possibilities before they catch on, from the crumbling Soviet Union to Papua, New Guinea. "I am a firm believer in trying different sorts of experiments, popping in and out, seeing if you like it," LeBaron says. "If you like it, stay. If you don't, turn around and go out."

Flighty though it may sound, LeBaron's credo built Batterymarch into an investment management company with assets of $12.3 billion at the end of 1993. His original partners, Jeremy Grantham, Richard Mayo and Eyk Van Otterloo left in 1977 to form their own contrarian investment firm, leaving LeBaron the sole proprietor. From its founding in 1969, Batterymarch has produced a string of investment strategies and trading techniques that have kicked institutional investing toward the next century.

Willingness to experiment has garnered considerable personal wealth for Lebaron. After relinquishing some control of Batterymarch in recent years to allow more time for contemplation, he still owns the lion's share of the firm's stock. Although the magnitude of his wealth is kept private, the trappings are obvious. At various times he has owned jet planes, homes in Boston, New Hampshire and Switzerland, thousands of acres of U.S. farmland, plantations near Papua, New Guinea, and dozens if not hundreds of electronic gizmos—including an amphibious car and a grand piano converted into a computer-driven player piano.

When sitting still, LeBaron gives an impression that he is moving at high speed. His mind constantly checks out ideas that stream in unfiltered. It is almost a digital mode of thinking, without gaps. Every nanosecond carries a bit of new information. He seems capable of several coherent thoughts at a time, and jumping the track is a conversational hazard. "You could be talking about zebras and then he starts talking about the two-cylinder engine," says a close friend, Fabienne Olivier. "I think he has to rein it in or he would be going in 100 directions at once."

LeBaron is charismatic. Speeches, which he enjoys making and seldom prepares, grab audiences or, if he's in a cranky mood, antagonize them. Listeners are drawn to the rambling, idiosyncratic mix of humor, crankiness, enormous intelligence and a relentless aversion to conventional thinking. He is a skillful prop handler when he speaks. He makes a point of fining himself one dollar every time he says Leningrad instead of St. Petersburg, the new old name for that major Russian city. After watching LeBaron fine himself a few times, one wonders if it is really a slip of the tongue or a sight gag that works.

He has traveled to the ends of the earth, literally, to seek fresh perspectives. "A key reason why I went to Papua, New Guinea, was to learn about the outer fringe, what economies are like in areas where I have absolutely no knowledge whatsoever. Papua was the farthest place I could imagine. I lived there intentionally for the purpose of seeing what the outer fringe was like. Switzerland (where he likes to go to ruminate) is not the outer fringe."

He went to Papua for education and experience, he claims, not to make money—notwithstanding his investment in the copra plantations. He tried to mingle with the local business community, and even dabbled with the ways that native workers were organized to see whether it actually improved productivity. It didn't. But he did conclude that someone entrepreneurially inclined could find five opportunities a day to make a million dollars in New Guinea. He even tested one of them.

"There was a great opportunity to sell popcorn," he says, "because everybody sat around the village fire at night telling stories. So here you have people sitting around for about four hours after sundown and there is a fire in the middle. If you happen to have been in America and discovered that there is more money made in movie theaters selling popcorn than selling movies, and really the movie was the way to attract people to the popcorn stand, it is not terribly hard to figure out that really what you want to do in Papua is sell popcorn."

On two nights LeBaron traveled from bonfire to bonfire selling popcorn and teaching people how to make it. He claims he was very successful, but be that as it may, he carted the sandwich bags of popcorn around and offered them for 10 cents each. The popcorn came from the States, in anticipation of this culinary exercise. Demonstrations always accompanied the sales pitch. Since most people chewed beetle nut, a mild home grown narcotic, he tossed one in with the popcorn although it had no effect that he could discern. But the corn sold better with the beetle nut. The corn would pop, like magic, and like the medicine man of old, he rang up sales.

"They must have thought we were crazy," says Fabienne, who accompanied him. There was master-capitalist Dean LeBaron in his pink tie-dyed shirt, selling popcorn by the sandwich bag. "For all the world to see he looks like he is lecturing at Harvard," she says. "But he's speaking pidgin describing popcorn to New Guinea natives." It was classic LeBaron— spontaneous, short-lived, using a visual and supplying a concise lesson with global implications. Never mind the detail that it would take a lot of 10-cent bags of popcorn per person to make a million dollars on an island inhabited by just over three million men, women and children.

Anything LeBaron does is apt to exhibit as much the qualities of P. T. Barnum as John Maynard Keynes. A French industrialist friend once asked him to make a keynote address at a goodwill gathering of French and German industrialists. This French friend had in his mind a plan to help heal prejudices still stemming from World War II, and he decided that LeBaron was just the chap to set the right tone. LeBaron did not give a lot of thought to his address until the night before. He settled on a famous Harvard case study: how snap, crackle and pop transformed a soggy, tasteless cereal into one of America's most successful breakfast products. An actual sample of Rice Krispies, discovered by chance in the vast pantry of the Frenchman's Normandy chateau, supplied sound effects that leaped over language barriers and illustrated one of LeBaron's favorite tenets: that sitting back and letting information trickle down will produce better results than setting expectations and suffering disappointment when they fail to materialize.

For another offbeat view, take a weighty topic closer to home: LeBaron's provocative, if not-entirely-serious proposal for improving pension management.

Pension funds have very long life spans, twenty to thirty years normally. Most investors accept ample evidence that equity returns over a long span are more variable, but greater than bond returns. Batterymarch, for example, puts about 95 percent of the funds it manages into stocks. But the typical pension fund, ostensibly designed to maximize long-term performance, rarely puts more than 60 percent of its assets into stocks.

An asset allocation exercise cannot abide both pieces of information and still assume that investors are rational, LeBaron concludes. If pension funds have a long-term horizon, why would they be anything other than fully invested in stocks—and take the short-term lumps? Who cares what happens in between? But that is not the way conventional pension managers behave.

The way they do behave suggests that institutional investors have only a brief time horizon. Back out the accepted rates of return for equity and solve for duration, LeBaron glibly declares, and you come out with a three- to five-year life span. Why is it, he asks, that pension managers shrink an actuarial horizon of twenty to thirty years, and behave as if it is three to five years? One explanation, says LeBaron, is that typical pension managers spend fewer than five years in that job. Their attitude is, "I'd better not let anything happen in my three- to five-year time horizon, otherwise I will get fired or I won't become assistant treasurer."

What is the expected cost if that assessment is correct? Pension plans and shareholders (who ultimately foot the bill for underfunded plans) forgo very high returns in order to provide career insurance for the people involved in exercising the investment function, according to LeBaron. Alternatively, he proposes a novel form of career insurance for pension managers. They can do whatever they want in their tenure. If they hit home runs it's great for the beneficiaries and great for their careers. But if they fall below the line, and fail to perform after three to five years, they get fired and insurance kicks in, paying their salaries henceforth, adjusted for inflation. Premiums would not amount to much, LeBaron says, compared to the billions of dollars sacrificed when pension funds are managed with self-serving, short-term horizons.

This cantankerous manner of thinking keeps LeBaron out of step with the consensus—until it catches up to him. When it does, he'll do somersaults to distance himself again. "He out-contrarians contrarians," says Harvard Business School Professor Andre Perold, who wrote the first of several Batterymarch case studies in 1984. "When I see he's about to do something, I try to guess what it is he is going to do," Perold says. "Every time I guess, I guess wrong. After the fact, I look back. Not only did I not predict what he had done, it is clear that it was brilliant *and* contrarian." Perold attributes this ability to LeBaron's sixth sense about where the crowd is gathering and a distaste for being part of it.

Instead of seeking the reassurance of a crowd around him, LeBaron embraces embarrassment risk, a term coined by a Batterymarch colleague. The prospect of embarrassment, to LeBaron, is a positive sign. He flouts convention as a way to determine the truth *insofar as it can be determined*. "You have all of these forces putting you in the middle, particularly when you succeed. It is easier to change when you fail in the investment area," he says. "I like to change."

Much as he enjoys tilting against convention, LeBaron was not especially rebellious as a child. "He was not contrary at all," says his mother, Irene LeBaron. Little Dean, a model of obedience, did extremely well in school without any apparent effort, especially in anything mathematics-oriented. "He was always permitted to do what he wanted because he always wanted to do things we thought were correct," Mrs. LeBaron remembers. She insists that one of his more daring escapades was, in fact, apocryphal. He did not fly his father's plane to private school as a way of circumventing the ban on students' cars.

Mrs. LeBaron recalls only one fracas, over Dean's determination to play football. His father, a physician who spent World War II overseas, wouldn't hear of placing his son in a sport where serious injuries are legion. So Dean never got to don a helmet and shoulder pads. On the other hand, Dean did not follow in his father's footsteps. Blood made him think of butcher shops.

After Phillips Exeter Academy and later Milton Academy, which was closer to home, LeBaron went to Harvard with the class of 1955. He spent two years drinking and carousing before buckling down, more or less, to majoring in psychology and sociology.

Between his sophomore and junior years he got his first taste of professional selling. That summer of 1953 he was one of twenty-five volunteers recruited by the Vick Company, which made Vick's Vapo-Rub and other cold remedies. Vick was a top-drawer marketing company at the time, and the summer jobs attracted hundreds of applicants.

Two lessons stuck with LeBaron. One was a favorite of the company president, who liked to applaud the visionary who proposed enlarging the mouth of an economy size Vapo-Rub container. Why? Because inducing consumers to apply Vapo-Rub with three fingers, instead of two, increased wastage by 50 percent.

The summer's second lesson had a more meaningful impact on LeBaron's investment career. The setting was a poor neighborhood in Baltimore, where the young sales trainee had to prove his mettle before going off on his own to visit druggists in Georgia, Mississippi and Alabama—a territory not popular with veteran salesmen on hot summer days before automobile air conditioning. While his supervisor waited outside, LeBaron made his well-oiled pitch to an elderly couple who seemed ready to place a large order. Then he noticed that their shelves were well-stocked already. Some moments later he realized the problem. Both were deaf, and relied on well-meaning suppliers to fill the shelves when necessary. LeBaron's dilemma was clear: ring up a sale and graduate to his own territory, or tell his teacher that the store was sufficiently stocked with Vapo-Rub and hang up his order book.

"Few can understand now why I have been especially decisive in declining business opportunities that had attractive short run possibilities but were of doubtful long run value," he wrote later. "I have felt that brokers had as much obligation in serving their clients to recommend the sale of securities that they felt lacked merit as to recommend their purchase. I have recommended to some investment management clients that they look for other good firms when their interests do not coincide with our capabilities. These acts are not the expressions of someone who is intentionally shortsighted commercially, but rather the result of decision making by one who has returned to Baltimore many times looking for a small drugstore in the hope that he could buy back the $500 worth of Vick's products that must still be on the shelves."

After graduation from Harvard, LeBaron joined the Norton Company, in a personnel department that furthered his practical education in behavioral psychology. A year later he joined the Army and traveled to Germany, where he wound up running psychological tests used in leadership training of non-commissioned officers.

More elevated contrarian rumblings waited until Harvard Business School, where LeBaron observed that most case studies shared a common characteristic he calls the X factor. Class discussions lasted an hour and twenty minutes. Until the last ten minutes, the class reviewed details of each case. Students who had done a lot of very methodical work would present assessments based on well-reasoned but ultimately straight-line thinking.

Finally, in the last ten or fifteen minutes, professors would reveal some ingredient in the case that seemed relatively minor, but was the key to putting the whole case in a different light. As soon as the case was visible in that new light, the analyses moved in a different direction. The twist, or the *X Factor*, invalidated all the conventional discussion that preceded it. The common thread led students down one path, never the right path or the path that made evidence clear. "There was no right or wrong," LeBaron says. "But there was always a twist, a key. I was pretty good at finding those keys." He was good enough, anyway, to become one of the business school's prestigious Baker Scholars.

A summer job at White, Weld & Co., between LeBaron's first and second years at Harvard Business School, persuaded him to abandon lingering thoughts about a career in labor negotiations. What struck him about Wall Street was the fast pace and rapid response to decisions. He liked that a lot.

He also liked the Business School's courses in investment and the advice he received from a faculty member who appreciated LeBaron's rare analytical abilities. "Most people adopt their careers based on a rational analysis of their strength. So in your case, Dean," the professor counseled him, "maybe you ought to make a rational analysis of your weaknesses. The investment business is an area where you are making major decisions on the basis of flimsy information, frequently, in public, and subject to potential ridicule. You are wrong at least half the time, more likely more of the time, and you have to come back and do it again. Most rational people do not put their careers in the hands of such a capricious system. I think that might be right for you."

Duly forewarned, he joined F.S. Moseley & Co. after graduation in 1960. The stock market was motoring its way up at the time, propelled mainly by popularity of big growth stocks that came onto the scene in the late forties and fifties. LeBaron followed electronics stocks, which were in the foothills of a major market surge. Six months after he arrived, Moseley's research manager left to join Gerald Tsai at the burgeoning Fidelity Fund, and LeBaron was tapped to build Moseley's research department. A few years later he left Moseley and joined Keystone, a mutual fund management company, as director of research.

His experience at Keystone, where he controlled about $22 million in commission business, fostered suspicions about the caliber of conventional money management. When he took on responsibility for commission distribution among Wall Street brokers, he noticed that a variety of people *who clearly did not know what LeBaron was doing* remarked anyway that he was doing a brilliant job. For the first month or so he accepted praise at face value. But after another month he discerned a re-inforcement system divorced from the actual quality of job performance. And if it was working on him, he had to figure it was working on others.

LeBaron started looking around for a more compatible view of investing and investment management. John Bennett, a friend who was then working for another investment firm, Putnam Management, introduced LeBaron to Humphrey Neill. Neill, the *Vermont Ruminator*, was a business writer who retired to Vermont and wrote *The Art of Contrary Thinking*, a mainstay of contrary investment philosophy. "It was a more systematic approach to things that made sense to me," LeBaron says.

Neill exhorted listeners to be contrary, to reject the obvious and to spurn crowds. Epigrams abounded in his writing. The central message, "When everyone thinks alike, everyone is likely to be wrong," displayed a special resonance during the late sixties, when a handful of celebrated go-go mutual fund managers appeared to have the Midas Touch. Instantaneous gratification defined much of the tumultuous Kennedy decade, in communications, in fast foods, in space travel. In the stock market, so-called performance stocks delivered instant gratification by doubling or tripling like magic as frenzied investors scrambled to get rich quickly.

When LeBaron and three partners started Batterymarch in 1969, institutional investors were just beginning to assert their dominance in the stock market. It had been only about ten years since a handful of pension funds began investing in stocks for the first time since the 1929 Crash. Methods of money management were designed mainly for individual investors, hand holding approaches without any scientific approach to the kind of asset allocation that institutions now require. Batterymarch introduced pension funds to the Capital Asset Pricing Model (CAPM), an efficient market approach to stock evaluation too novel then for Keystone and other established money managers.

"Institutional investment techniques as I was practicing them and others were practicing didn't make any sense," LeBaron says. "There had to be something better. And then I engaged in what was, at least for me, a quest to find something better, and may have found it, at least then. But all ideas in the investment area, especially successful ones, decay. And people don't like ideas to decay in business. This is a business in which tradition makes sense. You build up a marketing momentum, investment record momentum, momentum with consultants and clients. They understand what you do. There is a great desire to not change, and those rigidities do not appeal to me."

Along with innovative investment ideas, Batterymarch introduced computers and cut transactions costs, a strong selling point especially in days of fixed commissions. The fledgling firm put its clients into stocks with small- to medium-sized market capitalization, a decidedly contrarian, non-institutional category at the time. Results glistened for two years. In 1970, Batterymarch rang up a 14.8 percent return on investment, beating the S&P 500 by more than 10 percentage points. The next year Batterymarch clients saw their investments increase 21.6 percent, more than 6 percentage points better than the market. Batterymarch was on the map, but still hard to find. In 1973, the firm managed $42 million for forty-one clients, not the major league yet.

Performance cooled off in the next two years as investors pushed aside small- and medium-sized stocks and embraced the Nifty Fifty. Batterymarch did no better than the market in 1972; in 1973 the firm fared somewhat worse than the market, which sank 20 percent. LeBaron felt his methodology was on trial and Batterymarch in the balance. He began keeping count of the number of days the firm could survive at the current rate of cash outflow. Tottering between success and failure, he took refuge by writing *Ins and Outs of Institutional Investing*, a self-appraisal of his unorthodox views on investing.

The young firm's outlook improved before cash ran out, thanks in large measure to indexing. Cooked up by academic theorists, indexing attracted Batterymarch, Wells Fargo, and American National Bank at about the same time as a vehicle for matching average returns in the stock market. It was the outgrowth of an efficient market theory that said, in the long run you can't beat the market, so why not match it for much lower transaction costs?

Index funds hold a substantial portion of institutional portfolios today, but at first they were not an easy sell, even though many large institutions were quietly using some ad hoc form of indexing already. Selling the idea of a systematized approach under outside management was different. How could a professional money manager go to a client and ask for fees just to match the market? Moreover, LeBaron notes, active investment managers were handy to have in bad times to point a finger at. Pension managers who anchored portfolios to the market, on the other hand, could sink right along with it.

Seeing beyond reservations to a chance to snare big institutional customers, LeBaron went on the stump. "They would ask me, well, don't you have skills? I'd say yes, I do have skills to do better than the index. But that's investing in small stocks which you don't want to do because they're too scary. But if you want me to invest in big stocks, I'm better off investing in an index than somebody else." In addition, Batterymarch focused on the cost efficiency of indexing, charging customers a fraction of the fees that active money managers collected. The spiel worked. Institutions began to see the light, with the anticipated effect. By the end of 1977, Batterymarch was managing more than $1 billion. It was in the big leagues.

Six years later, after assets under management surpassed $8 billion, LeBaron took Batterymarch out of the booming indexing business. Efforts to customize indexing programs had not caught on. Unlike competitors who have stayed in the fray, Batterymarch indexed only the top half of the S&P 500, which make up about 90 percent of the whole group's market capitalization. The lower 250 stocks were actively managed. It seemed logical, but fiduciaries were not interested in replicating performance by selected stock groups. They wanted the garden variety S&P index that everyone except Batterymarch was pushing.

LeBaron concedes that his fine tuning may have been a mistake. He thought incorrectly that savings in transaction costs would matter more to pension managers than routine fluctuations in a long-term investment program.

"We missed the index by small but consistent amounts. We said who cares? As a ten-year strategy you'll make it back. The main thing," says LeBaron, "we were not spending transaction costs to chase this relatively small amount of the component of the index we didn't have. That was wrong. Because as the number of indexes became more common, the only way to discriminate one indexer against another was by tracking. So it became a great tracking mania. How close are you, month by month, to tracking the index—which I thought was an irrelevant measure. I still think it's an irrelevant measure. I said, this is getting ridiculous. It's just a marketing game. There is nothing we are doing here that is any better or any worse than we do elsewhere. We left it."

Besides indexing, the 1970s brought forth a tide of innovation at Batterymarch. The decade featured a long string of investment strategies that broke the mold of conventional stock picking. Instead of selecting stocks in the usual way, Batterymarch defined promising investment themes. Some sounded fairly pedestrian, like large high-yield stocks or depressed growth stocks. A few sounded rather exotic— financial cannibals (companies with substantial stock buyback programs) or hate group (stocks other investors wouldn't touch). Other categories included cyclical opportunity, financial tension, unrecognized assets, and raw materials. All told Batterymarch tested fifteen different themes by 1985. They did not all pay off in high

returns, but those that did at least secured for LeBaron his reputation as an outstanding innovator.

Inventing broad themes and filling baskets with stocks that
fit came naturally to LeBaron, the former electronics analyst
who told *Business Week* in 1976, "My idea of the future investment management organization is a few senior people and one
big machine." While competitors were beginning to use computers for crunching the same old numbers, LeBaron put them
to much more imaginative use in designing strategies and executing them efficiently.

Long before program trading was even a term anyone used,
Batterymarch broke ranks with other investment managers and
began giving brokers "sunshine lists" of stocks for purchase or
sale. Normally, handing that information to brokers exposed
the investment manager to the perils of front running. The broker could squeeze some extra profits by trading the stock for its
own account before executing the customer's trade.

But Batterymarch enjoyed built-in protection against front
running. A broker cannot exploit his customer's order if the
customer can trade another stock through another broker and
then withdraw the first one. Since Batterymarch was interested
in characteristics, like companies engaged in proxy fights, sub-
stitutions were routine. At the same time, brokers refrained
from burning good customers whose requirements were com-
plementary. When orders came in, traders were flexible on
price but inflexible on names. Batterymarch was just the opposite, flexible on names but inflexible on price. And as contrari-

ans, the folks at Batterymarch usually had an appetite for buying stocks others were selling, and vice versa.

Trading and investment strategies hinged on computer capabilities, and LeBaron fell in love with computers. It followed from his instinctive grasp of mathematics and physics. "It's something you can understand at an intuitive level without understanding on a mechanical level," he says. "I can catch it right away." He dreams of finding enough time to complete a book connecting investment thinking and quantum mechanics.

His collaborator on the book, Keith Johnson, teaches quantum physics at the Massachusetts Institute of Technology. "If Dean had more time he'd have made a very good scientist," Johnson says. "But he'd have been a generalist, not a specialist. He would have been thinking in a general way about forging new ideas." As it is, Johnson says LeBaron understands concepts that evade some of his fellow physicists. LeBaron is fascinated, for example, with chaos theory, which suggests a kind of internal structure in randomness, and its application to investing.

"It would be good to have a whole new precept, [that is] the reason I'm interested in chaos," LeBaron says. "Everything that operates in the United States operates on the assumption that the investment business here is linear and continuous. That's not true. The world is not that way, the world is non-linear, it is complex, and it is discontinuous. It may well be that failure of forecasting, failure of performance measurement is based not so much on the fact that people are dumb but that they are subject to Heisenberg's uncertainty principle." LeBaron is intrigued by Werner Heisenberg, the early 20th century physicist who showed that it is impossible to observe light without distorting the experiment.

Likewise, in the stock market, an observer is inseparable from experiment. Investor psychology turns the market from bullish to bearish, and back again. LeBaron the contrarian watches participants, not necessarily the economic data. There are limitations, however, in the real world. An expensive effort to program computers to scan newspapers for negative or positive words, for example, did not produced a meaningful result. "I don't know why not," LeBaron says. "Maybe we're not smart enough." He is certain, though, that comfortable approaches are wrong. "All we are doing is learning more about the observer," he says. "It seems that you have got to break out of that cycle, and the way to break out is to develop a new set of mathematics."

Now that LeBaron has turned over the CEO reins to a successor, Tania Zouikin, he has more time on his hands to seek a new set of mathematics. He recently bought an interest in a Swiss firm that comprises a handful of mathematicians, computers and theories about how chaos plays out in the stock market. This sort of activity fulfills LeBaron, but freedom to indulge curiosity comes at the cost of letting the firm he founded find an identity of its own. Without LeBaron actively in charge, Batterymarch is decidedly less contrarian. There are executive titles and office doors and a visible pecking order that did not exist when every executive was a trustee, a title stemming from the firm's legal structure as a Massachusetts Business Trust (set up with an eye to succession in case LeBaron departed the picture unexpectedly).

LeBaron no longer calls Batterymarch his personal sandbox, a place comfortable for him and fine for others who happen to find it comfortable also. Despite freeform ways, Batterymarch was never infinitely tolerant of anyone like LeBaron, except, of course, LeBaron. "If the organization is going to be designed around being deviant in some way, not in a bad way I hope but deviant nonetheless, it can't have multiple or conflicting deviance," he says. "You can't have a bunch of people bouncing around, particularly if they are intellectually strong. It is unlikely that you would get two people or three who have relatively off-the-wall ideas sitting down and agreeing with one another for any long period of time."

Batterymarch has given LeBaron credibility and a soapbox, which he freely exploits. It has opened doors between academia and the real world. Since 1980, Batterymarch has been patron to three academic researchers each year, supplying office space and a handsome stipend. Topics run the gamut from more or less practical (*How Many Stocks Make a Diversified Portfolio* and *Inefficient Dynamic Portfolio Strategies or How to Throw Away a Million Dollars in the Stock Market*) to comparatively esoteric (*On Correlations and Inferences about Mean-Variance Efficiency* and *Optimal Aggregation of Money Supply Forecasts: Accuracy, Profitability, and Market Efficiency*). For the program's tenth anniversary, in 1990, Batterymarch published the full collection as *Frontiers of Finance*. LeBaron's foreword, explaining the program's genesis, starts in typical fashion: "The decision was made in a matter of five minutes."

LeBaron considers most paper work inimical to truly productive thought. He says that his best ideas come from free association and "letting the mind play." But for much of the last ten years, attending daily to Batterymarch and its customers interfered with letting his mind play. His preference for thinking over doing evokes an observation by the author Joseph Conrad in his novel *Nostromo*, the story of revolution in a small, silver-rich central American country: "Action is consolatory," Conrad wrote. "It is the enemy of thought and the friend of flattering illusions."

LeBaron's condominium in Switzerland supplies a haven that he escapes to as often as he can, usually two or three times a year. He fancies a kinship with Niels Bohr, Robert Oppenheimer and other quantum thinkers who retreated to the Swiss mountains to contemplate relationships in the universe they could not actually observe. Their famous *thought experiments* intrigue LeBaron. They relied on imagination because they were dealing in scientific theory that was centuries ahead of the tools at their disposal, adequate only to demonstrate Newtonian theories. LeBaron's own ruminations during two weeks alone in the summer of 1990 fell far short of cosmic importance, but they produced a set of maxims he calls *Thoughts While Not Shaving*.

Kooky or profound, *Thoughts While Not Shaving* reveal the inimitable LeBaron. Some insights:

- There is too much liquidity and not enough investment.
- In the U.S., investment technology counts for nothing, wisdom counts for everything.
- In the last twenty years, the right course was to be disciplined and steady; in the next ten years—be firm in the conviction that you will only know a few things; they will change and be short term.
- A time series is a fallacy.
- Neutral is uncommitted.
- Time is an enemy to investors.
- The economic chain is too complex with too many levels and has too many uncommitted agents.
- Institutional investment organization is the Achilles heel of success.
- After a decade of risk management dedication and an unprecedented bull market, we will have a decade of reward management concentration and a bear market.
- The goal is real absolute terms, not relative performance.
- Make volatility of events and markets your ally.
- Mistakes of commission have the same character as triumphs.
- If you are complacent about your investment decisions, they are wrong.

- Unless you become right within twenty-four months, you are wrong.
- Be an investment guerrilla; strike back fast, unpredictably...and withdraw.

The question Batterymarch clients must ask is whether LeBaron can translate these thought fragments into a consistently successful investment strategy. Investment returns have not always matched the level of LeBaron's prolific imagination. Remembering his view of career insurance after several years of frustrating under performance, one is tempted to ask him why Batterymarch did not retire from managing U.S. equities during a long, disappointing slump in the late eighties and early nineties, from which it has since emerged.

LeBaron traces that slump to a misguided decision that value investing, defined by low-price earnings multiples and high yields, was the new consensus. That dashed it for him. As an annual report eventually explained, "It is easy for us, as contrarians, to respond; we do not rely heavily on conventional valuation rules. We expect the value investing mania, like all fads, to eventually end. If, as we anticipate, widely used valuation tools lose their predictive power, conventional value investing will no longer produce superior returns." Switching to anything *except* value investing did not work, however. Good ideas were scarce in contrast with earlier years. Nothing gathered favorable momentum, and performance continued to slide. Meanwhile, the ebullient bull market continued to reward investors who stuck with the crowd.

After sadly under performing the S&P 500 in 1989, LeBaron canceled all vacations the following summer, hoping to regroup while clients were quiet. Few strategies emerged, none stuck. In the end, they settled on a conventional approach that is anathema to LeBaron, individual stock picking. Worse, LeBaron says with clear disdain, everyone picked mainly "blue chippy type growth stocks." It was a turning point, but not an auspicious one. "It was my way of saying I've done what I can. Whatever happens, happens, because people had it happen to themselves." As 1990 ended, U.S. equity investment was still in the rough. But in 1991, 1992 and 1993, the U.S. equity portfolios resumed their edge over the S&P 500. Investors who have stuck with Batterymarch from inception have enjoyed a 12.7 percent return, net of fees, versus an 11.3 percent gain for the S&P 500, adjusted for dividends.

Investment outside the U.S. has become the primary vehicle for LeBaron's contrary ideas. Batterymarch has plunged into one foreign market after another since 1979, when it set up a small but symbolic $50 million pool of capital devoted to investments abroad. Although U.S. multinational companies were drawing larger and larger earnings streams from other countries, institutional investors viewed direct foreign investment until recently as too risky—meaning unpopular and undervalued, as LeBaron reads that information. At the end of 1993, investments outside the U.S. represented almost 60 percent of the funds Batterymarch managed.

The first actively managed foreign portfolio began operation in May 1983. A year later Batterymarch was active in eighteen markets outside the U.S., principally Europe, Japan, Hong Kong and Mexico. By the end of 1985, the non-U.S. equity portfolio neared the $1 billion mark. From inception through 1993, the Batterymarch International Equity Composite chalked up a gain of 29.8 percent, compounded. Though it lagged behind a 32.9 percent return by the benchmark EAFE Index, Batterymarch far outpaced a gain of less than 12 percent by the S&P 500.

To illustrate the firm's global reach, the cover of the 1989 annual report showed a map of the world skewed to each country's market capitalization. Two major contributors to the world's industrial production were notably absent: China and the Soviet Union. LeBaron has made it his mission to help put both countries onto the capitalist map.

The adventure that put LeBaron in the midst of the 1991 Russian coup d'etat started almost by accident during the previous summer. About thirty members of various Russian ministries, mainly allied to the military industrial complex, were visiting Boston in the hope of attracting investment. Their host invited LeBaron to address the group. He stole the show, says a friend who recalls the event. The Russians found LeBaron's freewheeling presentation refreshing. Seizing the moment, he invited them back to his home in Brookline that very night. The next day, one at a time, Russians began streaming into Batterymarch to talk with LeBaron about transforming military production facilities to commercial use. Within twenty-four hours, LeBaron put together a group of his own, and two weeks later he disembarked in Moscow, where a Dacha was put at his disposal.

Unpopular, undervalued, misunderstood, all those words apply to investments in Russia and the surrounding Commonwealth of Independent States. But, strange to say, LeBaron insists that investing there is not contrary at all. To his way of thinking, investing in Russia is trend-following in its most basic, pedestrian form.

One by one, he says, markets around the world have become economically intertwined. That trend could change, owing to trade barriers or revolution. But by and large, the trend has persisted for decades. LeBaron calls this an investment imperative. Opportunities abound for anyone with imagination and staying power. To be the first on the ground in absolutely open territory is an analyst's dream. The only thing against it is what is in our minds, that we have a mental image that is unlike the reality.

The analyst, the evangelist, the entrepreneur and the missionary all converged in Russia. "If you came down from Mars, or from the MIR space station after twenty years where communication has been like the Moscow telephone service—in other words, you don't know what is going on—and you were charged with the task of investing money, you wouldn't have a lot of baggage with you. What kind of investments would you make? I think you'd invest in the Soviet Union. It's one of those things that would seem obvious. Like investing in farmland. It is a big gap in the institutional framework. All you have to do is prove that it is not wrong for it to be done. If it is distinctly wrong then it shouldn't be done. But that is a hard burden to prove."

The Russian venture did not pan out as hoped, unfortunately. Even LeBaron's mighty powers of persuasion could not lift the veil of uncertainty that blinds most investors to exceptional opportunities. But the restless Batterymarch chairman does not second-guess himself. LeBaron moves on toward the next opportunity. Fear of being wrong does not oppress him, in part because he has not decided what failure, or success for that matter, should look like. Being in flux liberates him. What matters most to LeBaron is the long list of friends and colleagues he has gained from the Russian experience. He is an optimist. "We can go back," he says proudly, "any time we wish."

Chapter Two

*M*OST CONTRARIANS ENJOY FREEDOM TO ACT UNOBSERVED, *shielding themselves from the harsh light of skeptical crowds. But John B. Neff has operated in a fishbowl since 1964 as manager of the Windsor Fund. His performance is an open book, scrutinized continually by thousands of mutual fund investors. But who can complain? Neff's "lean-against-the-wind" philosophy has delivered superior returns over the long haul.*

John B. Neff

The Very Model of a Modern Money Manager

"*T*HE THING THAT CHAMPION INVESTORS CAN DO," SAYS JOHN Neff, an indisputable champion himself, "is get on the other side of their enthusiasms." They may want to believe something else, but great investors can leave their expectations behind in order to judge coldly the worth of an investment decision. Although somewhat awkwardly put, this spontaneous insight pleases Neff. His voice changes pitch, his gestures quicken and he puts his foot up on a chair, all as if to say, *that's it, that's the ticket.*

The shingle Neff envisions, if the celebrated Windsor Fund manager ever goes into business for himself, is "Fundamentals with a Flair." His wife, Lilly, says it sounds too feminine, but Neff clearly likes the succinct statement of an investment approach that has far outpaced the stock market since 1964.

Windsor has prospered by shunning investor fancies. Neff's lean-against-the-wind approach stresses good investment fundamentals in companies outside the current spotlight. Here's how he depicted the strategy for shareholders in the 1974 annual report: "Windsor Fund tends to be a 'contrarian.' In other words, we're not reluctant to invest meaningful sums in stocks of undiscovered, misunderstood, or neglected areas where we think the intermediate term outlook is good, and the price is favorable."

Bull markets, bear markets, transitional markets, oil shortages, double digit inflation, performance investing, the Nifty Fifty, leveraged buyouts, the 1987 crash—none has compelled Windsor to veer from a contrarian path. Dull though its portfolio often appears, the results glisten. Since 1965, it has beaten the market twenty-two times, averaging 13.2 percent a year. Total return on investment has exceeded 20 percent no fewer than thirteen times, and fell just shy in 1993 with a 19.1 percent return—far exceeding a 9.8 percent increase by the S&P 500 index. Four times, the total return has climbed past 30 percent. Meanwhile, Windsor has chalked up a stunning 2,067.2 percent return, nearly double the S&P index. In transforming a $10,000 investment at inception to $216,722 at the end of 1993, Windsor has proven that a large, diversified mutual fund can move nimbly enough to outpace a supposedly efficient market.

Neff embarked on this contrarian path as soon as Windsor's shell-shocked directors tapped him to rescue the $75 million Fund from a two-year tailspin. When he arrived, in 1964, Windsor was one of two mutual funds under the umbrella of Wellington Management. The flagship Wellington Fund, formed in 1928, survived the depression by clinging to a balanced mix of fixed income securities and sturdy blue chip stocks.

Windsor started life in 1958 as the closed-end Wellington Equity Fund. Steered by an investment committee, the fund caught the crest of a surging boom in big growth stocks. But the committee was slow to react when most investors hopped off the growth bandwagon in 1962. The sluggish response cost Windsor shareholders one fourth of their investment in a year when the market was off less than 9 percent. When the market roared back a year later, Windsor lagged along at barely half the pace. "It was so bad," Neff recalled, "they said at least make it neutral."

He did far more, but not without some resistance at first. Neff's rescue plan featured a novel proposal. Instead of chasing fashionable stocks on the way up, why not stake out positions in "adrenaline" groups before the crowd caught on to them? To directors obsessed with safety, going against the crowd sounded risky at first. But Neff soon convinced them that popular stocks posed more downside risk than holding out-of-favor investments in companies with sound credentials and low market evaluations.

"Solid citizens" still form the core of the Windsor portfolio:

- Price-earnings ratios well below that of the general market;
- Demonstrated or provable fundamental [earnings] growth of 7 percent or better;
- Yield protection in about 40 percent of this segment;
- Clear understanding of the company's franchise and the customer's need for the product;
- Record of persistent annual increments of earnings virtually without interruption.

Neff stresses total return, not growth only. Other investors normally assign higher price multiples to companies with lofty growth rates than to companies with modest growth rates and robust current yields. The tendency puzzles Neff, who would rather bank on the dividend and a rate of growth that is easier to sustain and likely to improve. His stock in trade is usually a company with earnings growth of 7 percent to 10 percent a year plus a 5 percent to 7 percent yield, for a total return which maybe yields 14 percent, all told, at six or seven times earnings. Typically, these are second-tier companies in promising industries—for most investors, the wrong side of the tracks.

But Neff is not rooted to any single approach, not even his own, when a good stock is out of favor. His biggest home run, Tandy Corp., had no yield in the years that Windsor owned it, from 1973 to 1981. Home Depot, another big hit, was a little out of character. Measured by slumping earnings in 1985, Windsor paid a steeper-than-usual P/E multiple. "But it was cheap on what we thought were normal earnings, once it could go through this stage," Neff says. "And we were absolutely right. We must have made 70 percent."

The decidedly contrarian approach reversed Windsor's fortunes in Neff's first full year as portfolio manager. The total return was 29 percent in 1965, more than twice the return for the S&P 500. In each of the next five years, Windsor chalked up hefty gains when the market went up, and softened the blows when it retreated.

Like other top-flight investors, Neff relies on a lot of basic analysis performed by an able staff. Chuck Freeman, assistant portfolio manager, joined Windsor in 1969. Two senior portfolio analysts, Jim Averill and Jim Mordy, add sharp perspectives that have lifted returns in recent years, Neff says.

But exhaustive number crunching by associates could not have produced Windsor's track record without Neff's special gift: an eye for detecting inflection points invisible to investors in the clench of crowd psychology, or group think. Obvious in retrospect, group think exhibits remarkable resilience. "It's an extension of what has happened already as though it is going to continue to do that in the future for ever and ever and ever," Neff observes. "Yet companies change, more importantly, industries change and trends change." Where others see peeling paint, crumbling plaster and leaky pipes, Neff sees rejuvenation and a hefty return on investment.

"The thing that most surprises me is how short people's memories are," Neff says. "You'd think with the advent of computers, with MBAs and with modern portfolio theory, the marketplace would not give you the wide vicissitudes of opportunity and overvaluation that you keep seeing. But if anything, it gets worse. It seems as though the markets are complete captives of momentum."

Much is often made of Neff's casual manner and midwestern values as if they explain his aversion to glitz and glamour. To all appearances, success has not infected him with high anxiety or overbearing self importance, or at least he hides those traits well while chatting in his third floor, corner office in Berwyn, Pennsylvania. He often answers his own phone. There are no troops of eager, self-important underlings catering to him and casting sneering glances at unfamiliar visitors. Talk about investing, and Neff will use words with an informal, most un-Wall Street ring: good companies are "solid citizens," companies that lost their following are "woebegone," residential real estate developers are "sticks builders," and "on the squash" describes stocks under selling pressure.

After Windsor suffered a horrible drubbing in 1973, Neff's annual letter to shareholders invoked words of a kindred spirit, Benjamin Franklin. "Be honest; toil constantly; be patient. Have courage and self reliance. Be ambitious and industrious. Have perseverance, ability and judgment. Cultivate foresight and imagination." A year later, perseverance paid off. Windsor's total return on investment streaked to more than 54 percent, outpacing a red hot S&P 500 benchmark by more than 17 percentage points.

Observers who know Neff well offer additional reasons for his enduring success. "You can write about style all you want," says Windsor Director Burton G. Malkiel, Chemical Bank Chairman's Professor of Economics at Princeton University and the author of *A Random Walk Down Wall Street.* "What distinguishes John from other people is that he really is an incredibly hard worker. He just has knowledge about an incredible number of things, and not a superficial knowledge, a deep knowledge," Malkiel says. "If it's a situation I know particularly well, I ask him a question and he amazes me."

The first time they met, Neff displayed a dazzling command of government data and its limitations. His fresh insights were quite a shock to Malkiel, who had just served on the President's Council of Economic Advisors, as chairman of an intergovernmental agency working on ways to improve statistical systems.

"Contrarian is right. You could also say cranky and humorous, certainly independent and intelligent. He doesn't buy what is faddish or hot on Wall Street," says Alan Abelson, former editor of Barron's and moderator for the annual investment roundtable that has included Neff since the Seventies. Neff, Abelson notes, tends to concentrate investments far more than roundtable colleagues like Peter Lynch, the former manager of Fidelity's super successful Magellan Fund. "Peter was someone who believed in buying everything that moved, filling a portfolio with a couple of thousand names," Abelson says. "John can take $4 billion or $5 billion and invest in fewer stocks." Case in point: When California real estate felt financial tremors in the fall of 1990, Windsor snapped up 6.5 percent of home builder Kaufman & Broad. Six months later, a buyer took the whole position for twice Windsor's cost.

"He has his weaknesses," Abelson says. "Stubbornness, possibly staying longer with things than he should. But if you wanted to go away for two years and forget about your money you could leave it with him and feel safe."

It is hard to say where Neff's contrarian roots took hold. He was always an outsider, even in his hometown of Corpus Christi, Texas. He was a lousy student, he says, unless goaded to perform by a teacher's insult. His parents divorced when he was in school, his father moved out of state. Neff, his mother and his sister continued to live a comfortable, middle class existence. Though not especially rebellious, he seldom took things at face value. His mother often shrugged that her son would argue with a signpost.

A high school diploma in hand, Neff wasted no time before heading north, to Ann Arbor, Michigan, where he took a job in a juke box factory. But that only lasted a few months before his father plucked him away from the music business and introduced him to the stock market.

"He had me invest my savings in kind of a family company," Neff says. Aero Equipment, then listed on the American Stock Exchange, distributed air-driven equipment for industrial and automotive uses. Better yet, and this still amuses Neff, his father offered to make up any losses. But the elder Neff could not make up for lost time, and working together didn't pan out. After five months, they called it quits. "He was not an easy man," Neff says. "And of course he'd say I wasn't an easy son, either. And his business didn't exactly fascinate me." Years later, however, Neff would find it harder to resist companies in unfashionable businesses.

Neff drifted into the Navy in January 1951. All told, Neff figures he spent 14 months of his two-year hitch in classrooms, of all places, mainly studying aviation electronics. "I wasn't an electronics wonder," he concedes. Meantime, he decided to go to college. After his discharge he enrolled at the University of Toledo. By choosing industrial marketing as his major, Neff received credit for long hours spent over military electronics manuals. As electives outside industrial marketing, Neff selected courses in investment and corporate finance.

Finance captivated Neff, thanks in no small measure to Professor Sidney Robbins. An early disciple of the legendary Benjamin Graham, Robbins introduced Neff to Graham's principles of securities analysis. "I kind of took to it," Neff says in a typical, understated fashion. More than just teach finance, Robbins sparked a career-shaping revelation. "Until Dr. Robbins persuaded me otherwise," Neff says, "I never really thought that you could do all in the investment business unless you came from an old family or went to an Ivy League school."

But a chilly reception awaited Neff as he hitchhiked 400 miles between Cleveland and New York just prior to his graduation in January 1955. Far from welcoming an eager fellow from Ohio with an unorthodox background, Wall Street's old boys displayed no interest. No one picked up an expensive hotel bill; Neff paid his own tab at the YMCA. He approached Merrill Lynch, Blyth Eastman Dillon and Smith Barney, whose training programs were featured in an issue of *Barron's*. None offered to train him as a stock broker. Bache, a somewhat smaller firm where Robbins worked in the 1930s and still carried some weight, offered Neff a job, but not the one he wanted. A voice lacking in authority ruled out becoming a stock broker, so Bache offered to make him a securities analyst.

If he was going to become a securities analyst, however, Neff could do that without leaving Cleveland, where there was an opening at National City Bank. Staying put also suited Neff's wife, a midwesterner with no fondness for big city lights.

An early colleague, Arthur Boanas, remembers word circulating that National City's trust department was about to get a new recruit, fresh from college. When Neff showed up, he was inexperienced but not shy or self-effacing. "I would say that he was full of himself more than full of ideas," says Boanas, a British emigré. Nevertheless, the two men discovered common attitudes toward investing, chiefly a disdain for conventional thinking.

Besides exposing Neff to the "fearsome responsibility" (as he puts it) of managing other people's money, eight years at the bank bolstered his contrarian instincts. "Maybe it was too prudent or too much hitting behind the ball," Neff says. The trust department bought industry leaders despite the compelling case that the stock market overvalued leadership and undervalued other good companies. "I wasn't given an ability to exercise a little imagination or creativity, or to take an intelligent risk."

Neff describes Boanas as "the brightest guy I've run across." Boanas recognized in Neff an exceptional dose of intellectual ruthlessness, the contrarian's life preserver. "When you have taken that tack, it's lonely," Boanas says. "It pits you against the rest of the investment community, which can make you look bloody wrong."

Windsor charts a lonely course by putting every detail on fact sheets, building price targets, then living and breathing off those targets. When a stock approaches its expectation, Windsor starts getting out. If that means sacrificing an additional gain of 10 percent, 20 percent or more, so be it. Neff never regrets selling too soon. Never court delusions of grandeur and don't play the greater fool's game, he warns. If anything elicits a ruthless side, it's situations where actual events fall out of bed with expectations. "You look at your model," Neff says. "If it doesn't work, then turn on it. We don't marry anything. Everything we own is for sale."

Moreover, Windsor usually accumulates stock on the way down and sells on the way up. "It's really the antithesis of what everybody else does," Neff says. "That's why the odds are so good—if you've got any conviction and any execution and any continuity. But most people can't do that. Each day you do, you are wrong versus what you did the previous day. That grates with some people. In a lot of cases, you've got somebody looking over your shoulder [saying], 'Christ, you dummy, why didn't you sell that yesterday when you could have gotten more today?'"

Buying on weakness and selling on strength automatically produces opposite reactions at turning points. Starting in 1990, for example, Windsor began accumulating shares of AMR Corp., the parent of American Airlines. By then, even good airlines were out of favor with investors, who feared the impact of declining passenger traffic. In February 1992, American announced an uptrend in passenger traffic. For most investors, that was a signal to start buying. Windsor began selling.

Success is not automatic, however. In 1984, for example, Windsor started buying shares of Ford Motor Company at bargain basement prices between $10 and $13 a share. Neff foresaw improved earnings, but he was not counting on a billowing P/E ratio. The market's wisest moments occur, he says, when it does not allow cyclical earnings to inflate multiples.

On the strength of robust earnings, Ford's stock rose sharply. But this time, Neff ignored the usual sell signals. Even after a fourfold increase in Ford's price, he sat tight. "We didn't sell a single share," he says, some dismay still apparent a few years later.

Ford notwithstanding, Neff insists that Windsor has never slackened its customary sympathy for selling a stock the market has embraced. Even at $56 a share, Ford still fell short of earnings expectations, and the ratio was still within Windsor's acceptable range. Moreover, Neff would have looked smart if Ford had not blindsided investors in 1989 by overpaying for Jaguar, the elite British car manufacturer.

Buying Jaguar at its peak of popularity was a monumental error, Neff reckoned immediately. Despite the Jaguar name and one of the few distinctive automotive shapes left, a $2.6 billion price tag was way too much for manufacturing facilities in desperate need of additional investment. Neff also doubted whether Ford executives really understood the nature of Jaguar's particular appeal and how it would stand up to increasing competition from Japanese car makers in the luxury category. By emptying its treasury of $2.6 billion in cash, Ford traded annual interest income of around $250 million for Jaguar's continuing operating losses. In 1993, Jaguar sold about the same number of cars as in 1989, and lost $371 million in the bargain.

Windsor started selling Ford shares as the price lost ground. When it cleaned out the last of its shares in early 1991, they fetched $33, a handsome premium over the acquisition cost but dismal next to what Windsor might have earned if it had been selling shares when the price approached the peak.

Though frustrating, Ford did not evoke the deeper soul searching that accompanied the Nifty Fifty era a decade earlier, when Windsor fell completely out of step with the market for three years running.

Like so many investment frenzies, the Nifty Fifty era was shaped by the frenzy that preceded it. Burned by ballyhooed startups and overextended conglomerates in the late sixties, investors converged on a handful of blue chip growth companies like Merck, 3M and Avon Products that promised to grow earnings around 15 percent a year, ad infinitum. One decision stocks, they were called. Supposedly, investors could hold them forever, enjoying steady double-digit growth rates in perpetuity, driven by earnings momentum and investor demand that outstripped supply. Price/Earnings multiples went ballistic. At fever pitch, bidders pushed the hottest stocks to more than fifty times earnings.

To Neff, these Nifty Fifty companies were monstrosities destined to collapse under their own weight. But it took longer than expected for the pendulum to swing back. The S&P average increased by nearly 35 percent in 1971 and 1972; Windsor lagged behind at barely half the pace. Those results only foreshadowed catastrophe in 1973, when the Nifty Fifty tumbled back to earth. Far from embracing Neff's solid citizens, investors bolted the market altogether. Trading volume collapsed and suddenly every decent big board company was lucky to fetch book value. The S&P tumbled 15 percentage points. Though carefully positioned to rise from the ashes of the Nifty Fifty, Windsor skidded 25 points.

For the first time, events rattled Neff's confidence. But not enough to persuade him to change course. Most investors who dwell in out-of-favor, woebegone stocks would be fools if not optimists. "When you go through these periods of market fancy for goods other than your own," Neff says, "you just have to wait it out—which is not always easy."

True to contrarian form, Neff raised the ante, betting that the next inflection point would turn events to Windsor's advantage. He dumped electric utilities, food companies, American Telephone, and other defensive investments. In came lesser known growth companies poised for a rebound. Many were selling for half their peak prices, and even lower, despite respectable earnings growth. A notch below, good companies on hard times crept along for 10 percent of their peak market values. Summing up 1973 in his report to shareholders, Neff promised that moves made that year would propel Windsor to record levels.

> For we view the current devastation in the marketplace, not as a reason for alarm, but rather as one of opportunity. We believe we will look back on this recent period of excessively low evaluations of innovative, accomplishing companies as one not unlike the early 1950s, when stocks of good companies also could be acquired at prices of only four or five times earnings—prices that provided the opportunity for truly remarkable appreciation in ensuing years.
>
> It is my view, as Windsor Fund's portfolio manager, that there is a period of outstanding potential appreciation on the horizon. As a shareholder with a substantial portion of my family's resources invested in the Fund—and one who has personally and financially lived and breathed each good day and each bad day with the Fund since mid-1964—I hope you await the inevitable eye-catching appreciation of our Fund with the same solid confidence and eager anticipation as I do.

The strategy began to deliver in 1974 by bracing Windsor against the market's steeper slide. As the market plunged almost 30 percent, Windsor only lost half as much ground. The next year brought vindication. In 1975, Windsor surged 54 percent, beating the market by 17 percent. Winners studded the portfolio: McLean Trucking (up 100 percent), Pizza Hut (up 136 percent), Edison Brother Stores (up 137 percent), Jonathan Logan (up 143 percent), White Consolidated Industries (up 172 percent), and Tandy (up 264 percent).

Tandy still ranks as Neff's longest home run. It was a classic contrarian play: earnings growth tracking up at better than 20 percent a year and a stock price 75 percent below its peak in 1973, when Windsor bought its first 50,000 shares for $17 a share. Accumulation continued for two years, usually on downticks, until consumer electronics started to lure investors. In May 1981, after the spin-off of Tandy's leather goods business and two two-for-one splits, Windsor sold its last 50,000 shares for roughly fourteen times the original purchase price. Around the same time Fortune magazine wrote glowingly of Tandy's prospects, but as it turned out, earnings soon stalled and the stock price went nowhere for a decade.

An end to the Nifty Fifty era marked the first of four major inflection points in Neff's career at Windsor. The second inflection took shape in 1980. Windsor trailed the S&P by nearly 10 percentage points while investors went wild over energy and technology stocks. Forbearance paid off the next year. Energy and technology stocks went south, leading the S&P down by nearly 5 percent. Windsor gained 16.8 percent, thanks to the blossoming of large positions in supposedly dull areas such as banks, foods, insurance, telephone and electric utilities. Luck also contributed. Soon after Windsor bought a large stake in

Conoco, as the price was falling, two bidders sought control. When chemical giant E.I. DuPont de Nemours finally bested Seagram's, a Canadian distiller, Windsor pocketed a $14 million gain.

Windsor edged out the market in 1982 and beat it solidly in the next two years, then stumbled in 1985. Though hampered by a growing cash position in 1986, in anticipation of a market correction, Windsor outperformed the market by a slim margin. Then came a third unmistakable inflection point, the 1987 Crash. At the time, 22 percent of Windsor's assets were in cash, not so liquid by hedge fund standards but for a stock fund like Windsor, the cash position pushed the limits of acceptability.

Neff was wary. "You had a lot of new issues and that hi-jinks," he says. "But the consensus says sure, the market is high, but you'll have plenty of time to get out. And I say, well, doesn't that mean that we won't have plenty of time? But I never imagined that it would essentially happen in one day." But the 500 point drop did not paralyze Neff, who proceeded to pour cash back into the stock market. By year end, Windsor was fully invested. It did not pay off, however, until 1988. Windsor's 30th year and Neff's 25th gave cause yet again for celebration. Windsor gained nearly 29 percent, to 16.5 percent for the market.

The formula appeared to lose some potency in 1989 and 1990. Disappointments were rife especially in 1990, when automobile holdings declined by 30 percent, airlines by 36 percent and insurance by 38 percent. Thumbnail critiques in the 1990 annual report underscore Neff's contrarian nature. On autos:

"Present prices have over-discounted the down cycle. Industry sales and Big 3 share will surprise consensus." On airlines: "Should be goodies in 1991, especially if oil does go back to low twenties." On Banks: "When the market [is] ready to discriminate again, we will make a lot of money on BAC, Bankers Trust, and Citicorp, which total 80 percent of our bank holdings." On Insurance: "Like the banks, we'll accomplish when the market stops broad brushing." Three groups delivered in 1991.

Airlines produced a 19 percent gain, insurance companies rose 45 percent, and banks nearly doubled. Autos, however, sank 2.1 percent. All told, Windsor beat the market again in 1991. The 5 percent margin was comfortable, though short of the "boxcar" gains that followed inflection points in 1973, 1980, and 1987.

In early 1992, Neff was gearing up for a rerun of the Nifty Fifty era, as investors chased after stocks of consumer non-durable companies on the misguided expectation that modest unit growth would continue forever. After a couple of underperforming years, he admits his reputation needed a lift. "I thought I might write a book after this," he said at the time, "although I'm going to have to do a little better. I'm not very commercial right now."

As predicted, consumer non-durables eventually went south once raw materials stopped dropping in price—a key factor behind such attractive returns. Windsor bounced back in 1992 with a robust 16.5 percent return versus 9.8 percent for the S&P 500. Big winners for the year included Citicorp, up 118 percent and British Steel, up 151.7 percent. Phillips NV was not so shabby either; its stock was up 89.8 percent.

"It happens and it happens and it happens," Neff says of the crowd's tendency to get carried away. "The ability of the stock market to overcapitalize a good thing runs amok," he says. But in almost the same breath, Neff warns that planning for identical reruns of market patterns can spell trouble also. "I've always said that he who worships at the altar of historical parallel does so at his clients' expense."

For this reason, Neff is reluctant to predict the next inflection point. But he doesn't doubt there will be one. As the first half of 1994 drew to a close, Windsor held large investments in a handful of commodities, including aluminum and natural gas—a sign that the stock market outlook was murky. But sifting through "pretty good internal carnage" still looked to Neff like a promising strategy. "We're still consistently dazzled by low P/E's," Neff says. The smart money says he's right on target again. Neff might put it another way: Every tub sits on its own bottom.

Chapter Three

THE MOST CEREBRAL OF CONTRARIAN INVESTORS, MICHAEL Aronstein brings rigorous intellectual discipline to a business where success usually reflects rising markets and short memories. Informed by a profound sense of history and a pessimistic outlook for financial assets, Aronstein's world view also illustrates the dangers of holding to a contrarian course when the tide is going the other way. But after enduring dark days right on the heels of brilliant success at Comstock Partners, Aronstein is now charting his own course. In West Course Capital, the investment firm he launched in late 1992, psychology, literature, value investing and classical economics converge on the rough and tumble world of commodities trading. Investors have not been disappointed.

Michael Aronstein

That Ain't Mud on Your Boots, Partner

ON THE LINKS AT THE WESTCHESTER COUNTRY CLUB, MICHAEL Aronstein is nearly as awesome as the giant clubhouse-hotel that is a throwback to the 19th century. He's a scratch golfer who might have earned a spot on the professional circuit if someone had taught him the proper way to grip a golf club. As it is, he has had to settle for top golfer at the keenly competitive country club and a volatile career on Wall Street, where an unorthodox grip fosters his iconoclastic outlook.

Golf magazine's former instruction editor argues that profligate use of credit ultimately breeds deflation, not inflation as conventional observers suppose. That is not good for owners of financial assets—the last bastion to withstand the tidal force of worldwide deflation. The current credit cycle will end the way every previous cycle has ended for 2,000 years, says Aronstein, with a default by the biggest borrower. It's unthinkable until it happens, and then it happens. When the wave hits, prices of financial assets will plummet. Contracts tied to these assets, from home loans to multi-billion dollar commercial loans, will transmit ill effects to the rest of the economy just as ill-conceived commercial loans played havoc with banks and thrifts.

"A market is a scale," Aronstein declares. "It just reflects the weight of belief." Prices, therefore, are pinned to nothing more palpable than expectation of what prices will be tomorrow. This is as true today, he warns, as when frenzied Dutch investors bid prices of tulip bulbs to stratospheric levels in the 17th century Tulipomania. Not only can it happen here, he says. It will. The wrecking ball is already in motion.

Critics consider Aronstein unduly pessimistic about the prospects for financial assets, but they acknowledge that the argument has merit. "Though it seems almost contra-intuitive, there is a chilling logic to it," *Barron's* reported in August 1989.

On the strength of his convictions, Aronstein surrendered most of his interest in Comstock Partners in 1992 to launch his own firm, West Course Capital—named for one of the Westchester Country Club's two golf courses. "The whole premise is to give people an alternative to forms of wealth storage that are now popular," he says. If the crowd wants financial assets, Aronstein reasons, then real value must lie somewhere else, namely, in commodities. So West Course Capital invests in commodities, but not in the fashion that commodities have come to be viewed by traders.

To Aronstein, commodities markets in 1994 resemble the bond markets in 1981 and 1982, after a thirty-year bear market drove out all players except hard core bond traders who live and die with each uptick or downtick. They focus on supply; Aronstein watches demand.

When intuition supported by exhaustive research persuades Aronstein to anticipate an upsurge in demand for a commodity—say lead, or cotton, or coffee, or even hemp—Aronstein invests long term, rolling contracts over at maturity rather than taking profits or losses at frequent intervals. It is a sort of Graham and Dodd approach to commodities, using many techniques of fundamental value investing. That this sounds odd to modern ears supplies one more piece of evidence that Aronstein is on the right track. Fundamental analysis with no companies? Says Aronstein: "Commodities are the most fundamental things. There are no treasury departments, no threats of tax increases. Commodities are the original concept of money."

Initial results support this offbeat concept. "So far, so good," offers Aronstein with characteristic respect for the vagaries of market behavior. In its first full year, 1993, West Course Capital generated a 15 percent return on investment, net of fees—outpacing the S&P 500 (adjusted for dividends) by five percentage points. Aronstein's biggest single investment was in coffee,

which he predicts will reverse a decades-long decline in consumption as baby boomers' increasingly forgo soft drinks—a
conclusion supported not least by the rapid proliferation of
cappuccino makers. More convincing still, the price of coffee
chalked up a 90 percent gain soon after Aronstein began to ac-
cumulate contracts. Nevertheless, Aronstein's investment style
won't ever win over most investors. It can't, by design. "I just
hope the wind is at my back," Aronstein says, "and then try not
to do what other people in my business are doing."

Aronstein fell out of step with other folks in his business almost as soon as he arrived on Wall Street in 1979. Small surprise, for a Yale graduate who wrote his senior thesis on the
poet Wallace Stevens. "Michael Aronstein, of the famed Comstock Partners, is extraordinarily bright, reflective and articu-
late," *Barron's* gushed in April 1992, "which always prompts
the question, 'What in the world is he doing on Wall Street?'"

Aronstein gives this explanation for an investment career:
"The whole process of financial analysis didn't intimidate me,"
Aronstein says. "I didn't see in reading the *Wall Street Journal*
and *Barron's* that there was a Wallace Stevens, where I would
say, 'Jesus, that's fantastic, but I can't write that way.' I didn't
see a Stephen Hawking (the acclaimed author of *A Brief History
of Time*). I looked and said I could compete in this field. It just
seemed to suit my way of looking at things."

He took his first job at Merrill Lynch, the giant wire house
that is almost a proxy for the crowd, after friends urged him to
join IBM, the only other employer willing to train him for a

management role. Merrill paid about half the starting salary, but Aronstein soon found ample compensation in a small group of like-minded colleagues. With Merrill veteran Stan Salvigsen as tutor, Aronstein expanded his intuitive understanding of the way financial markets operate. "[Salvigsen's] work in 1979-1980 was seminal," Aronstein says. "It agreed with things I had thought, but it was the first really rigorous exposition of long term credit cycles and long wave bond prices. It was instrumental in opening my eyes to how things worked."

As their collaboration progressed, Aronstein emerged as the expositor. His flair for expanding and articulating implications resulted in a series of economic analyses that were as fresh as their wacky titles: *The Big Enchilada; Homesick; Bingo, Bango, Bongo; Little Shop of Horrors; Snouts, Lips & Tails; Twin Peaks; 32ds Over Tokyo; That Ain't Mud on Your Boots, Partner,* to name a few. It was splashy marketing if nothing else. And from someone who lasted only six months in the public relations business before being fired for coming to work late.

Once it became obvious that their bearish outlook didn't jive with Merrill's bullish image, Salvigsen, Aronstein and a third Merrill colleague, Charles Minter, formed their own firm, Comstock Partners, in 1986. "We knew we wouldn't be able to talk about our view of the world," Minter says. "There is no way to run a large brokerage firm with a negative point of view."

Never mind that Comstock's contrarian analysis was grounded in the work of classical economists like J.M. Keynes and Ludwig von Mises, or that Salvigsen and Aronstein published dead-on predictions that sky-high prices for oil and commercial real estate were due for comeuppance. Or, for that matter, that they said that inflation was not as intractable as it seemed after almost two generations.

On their own, they quickly drew a following. They polished Comstock's fledgling image by pulling clients' money out of the stock market in August 1987, on the very day that the Dow Jones Industrial Average touched a high that it did not surpass again for several years. And then they weighed in with a timely prediction that spiraling prices for residential real estate would come to an abrupt end.

Visions of Armageddon suit Aronstein, an affable worrier with a poetic bent. In an era where most of his peers tend to trace their roots to Paul Samuelson and Milton Friedman, Aronstein is more of a renaissance type. Armed with a photographic memory, he has attacked the library of modern and classical economics without ever having taken a survey course in the subject. But he puts as much or more faith, at times, in lessons from literary giants like Wallace Stevens, whose treatment of disorder and renewal has plenty of resonance in modern finance.

These intellectual bearings seem odd if not wholly irrelevant on Wall Street today—in sharp contrast with past eras when finance was nearer the world of letters. Maybe, however, the kinship between finance and letters remains closer than most observers believe. Time will tell.

Deep-seated pessimism separates Aronstein from fellow contrarians, who usually are optimists as a necessary condition of their out-of-favor investment strategies. But if the last vestiges of wealth do go down the tubes, he is not likely to rub his hands and gloat. Like a modern-day Cassandra, who warned to no avail that tragedy awaited Agamemnon, Aronstein bears ominous tidings with considerable dread. He does not expect most people to pay attention. Nor, in any event, will paying attention reverse the trend. Fate has handed Aronstein a nasty job. The only question is, when to launch the lifeboats.

That's a tricky question, especially for contrarians. Lowering the life boats late is disastrous, of course. But lowering them too early also carries a stiff penalty, a lesson that Comstock Partners learned only too well in 1991. Convinced that bloated financial assets were in imminent danger of shrinking, Comstock stayed out of the stock market. Meantime, April 1991 saw the Dow Jones Industrial Average roar past 3,000 for the first time in history. Standard & Poor's 500 stocks gained more than 30 percent while Comstock barely eked out half as much for its investors. From a lofty berth in the universe of top tier institutional investment managers, the young firm crashed to less-than-average performance. The excruciating plunge highlights the soul-searching that sometimes lurks in wait for investors who chart a contrarian course.

Aronstein's dire predictions about looming deflation are linked to wealth creation, a core concept in capitalism. Each time a bank lends, it creates a new asset for itself and a corresponding liability for the borrower. But it does not create the means to pay interest costs. In early stages of a credit cycle, wealth resides in the hands of suppliers of commodities. Over time, the interest burden drains wealth from suppliers of commodities to suppliers of labor. Then, in the terminal stage, wealth ends up in the hands of the holders of financial assets. It's what Aronstein calls *Bingo, Bango, Bongo*. After inflation's final hurrah, the much touted magic of compound interest turns diabolical, working its effect on the liability instead of the asset. Instead of creating wealth, deflation destroys it.

Countries dependent on commodities in South America and Africa felt the deflationary wave first, as commodities prices swooned. The means of paying interest costs evaporated, but the accumulated debt remained—as if the balloon burst and left a corpus of debt resembling an indestructible Plexiglas block, too heavy to lift.

After toppling governments on southern continents, deflation moved north. It hastened an end to the Soviet Union, a giant, inefficient, third world-esque system highly dependent on commodities. "It starts with the weakest ones first," Aronstein says. "That's why I couldn't understand people here celebrating the collapse of the Soviet Union. It was like a miners' canary dropping dead when gas begins to leak in the coal mine. It should not be a point of amusement."

From the time he landed at Merrill Lynch, Aronstein sniffed something potentially explosive. Hired to become a stock broker, selling stocks made him uneasy. He could not persuade himself to cash in on investors' stunning capacity for overindulgence and self-delusion when it seemed clear to him that economic calamity lay straight ahead. No sooner did one pie-in-the-sky expectation come crashing down than another took its place. "It was amazing that this was the heart of the American financial system," he says, "and it was essentially run off grand misconceptions."

Misconceptions have centered on boundless expectations at every turn, from the Dutch tulip frenzy to clamorous demand for oil, real estate and common stocks more than 300 years later. Investors act as if booms go on forever, propelled only by insatiable appetites unmoored from common sense. Says Aronstein: "You look back at extremes and say, what were people thinking about?"

This puzzling behavior results from the natural human tendency to forecast more of the same. Just put the arrow on a trend line. Rear view syndrome, Salvigsen calls it. People react more strongly to their most recent experience whether or not common sense agrees that the extreme will repeat itself or become even more exaggerated.

In 1980, energy groups at major banks took on projects anchored by the flimsy assumption that oil prices would climb 10 percent to 15 percent a year for the next decade. Hardly had that bubble burst when home buyers and mortgage lenders persuaded themselves that home prices would climb ad infinitum, while commercial real estate developers produced spread sheets showing how commercial rents would increase for the next decade at 12 percent a year.

Aronstein often sat dumbfounded in the early eighties as "pretty smart people" on Wall Street jumped blithely on the milk wagon, saying "do you understand what you can do with these new conditions? That you could go out and just set up a savings & loan, pay an investment banker to raise $3 million, and then lend it to yourself to build condos?"

When banks unloaded those properties for 30 cents on the dollar, not an uncommon outcome after prices collapsed, it meant that initial projections were off by more than 300 percent—hardly within the bounds that anyone could call a reasonable mistake. The system works this way, Aronstein says, because repeated observation validates anomalies, no matter how far outside the pale. If enough people pay outrageous prices, then outrageous prices become the standards. But they are still outrageous. The music stops when the price becomes functionally ridiculous. "If it costs 75 cents to put a spoonful of sugar in your tea, you'll do something else. You'll have a glass of water and a pear."

This simple wisdom is rarely attractive when the crowd gets good and lathered. If investors had pondered seriously the implications of oil at $100 a barrel, they'd have concluded that Saudi Arabia would outstrip Japan as an economic force and Mexico would soon possess more wealth than Germany. Warning in 1987 that stock prices were vulnerable to the same deflation that swamped the oil business, Aronstein described the madness of crowds with his distinctive aplomb, in *That Ain't Mud on Your Boots, Partner.*

> When the oil boom neared its peak, companies in the business were paying young geologists fortunes to find and produce more and more oil. This is a little like the fellow assigned to shovel out the stables paying someone top dollar to come in and cook Mexican food for the horses. The inclination on the

part of businesses that are enjoying good demand
and pricing for their product to produce more of it at
higher and higher cost is the mechanism by which
supply eventually overwhelms demand and brings
down prices and profitability.

Viewing stocks in light of the oil collapse was not a casual
comparison. Extremes do not occur in isolation, according to
Aronstein. They are linked over long spans of time. In the closing decade of the 20th century, for example, society is captive of
a credit cycle with reflections in the era after the U.S. Civil War
and roots in the Great Depression.

In *A Short History of Financial Euphoria*, economist John Ken-
neth Galbraith described the bull market that followed the War
Between the States. It sounds eerily familiar, a post-war tale of
speculative boom that featured "pyramiding values and generally euphoric conditions in manufacturing, farming, and public
construction." Speculation focused in those days on railroads,
which seemed to enjoy limitless horizons. Lenders forgot about
defaults a few decades earlier, when canals and turnpikes captivated investors' imagination. Once more, harsh reality restored
them to their senses. "The new railroads, and some old ones,
could not pay," Galbraith wrote. "The respected banking house
of Jay Cooke & Company, heavily involved with railroad fi-
nancing, failed in September of 1873. Two large banks also
went under. The New York Stock Exchange was closed for ten
days. Banks in New York and elsewhere suspended payment in
hard coin."

This post-war tumult also featured double digit interest rates (which did not recur until the 1970s) and a rolling recession. Severe economic distress rippled from one economic sector to another, leaving in its wake a scorched trail of deflated prices. Some citizens enjoyed a boom while others muddled through a depression. Yuppies and poverty proliferated, side by side. It ended with the panic of 1873, from which the country did not recover for twenty years.

The credit cycle racing toward calamity a century later, in Aronstein's view, was born in the aftermath of the Great Crash. Hobbled by awful memories of 1929, the economy crawled or lurched through the thirties. By a long stroke this was Wall Street's most volatile decade. World War II brought a bull market, after which fear of depression resumed, fanned by the prospect of millions of unemployed servicemen.

So great was the angst in 1949 that common stocks yielded two and one-half times as much current income as bonds. Yet suggesting larger investments in stock would have cost most trust officers their jobs. Convinced that collapse was imminent, Montgomery Ward chief executive Sewell Avery reportedly refused to embark on an expansion-minded strategy. As a result, the once great retailer fell far behind its more adventurous cross-town rival, Sears Roebuck. Three decades later, Ward was a humble subsidiary of Mobil Oil Company.

Yet, in the late forties, actual conditions all but ruled out sliding back into depression. Liquidity and risk aversion prevailed, legacies of depression. Balance sheets were clean, swept free of frivolous investments. The government began introducing safety nets that would support economic growth. Bank loans amounted to a mere 20 percent of deposits. Everything consumers needed or wanted, including credit, was in abundant supply. With production operating at full tilt, the postwar era confounded expectations and produced unprecedented prosperity.

The government's increasing activism bestowed wonderful effects on the economy. The tax code stimulated borrowing. People took out loans for the first time to buy houses, cars and everything else that came with suburbanization. It was a wonderful confluence of forces, giving birth to the notion that credit was inexhaustible. Under President Johnson's administration, prevailing wisdom supposed that the government could use its access to credit to do whatever it wanted, without limit. But, as Aronstein sees it, expansion accelerated by the Viet Nam war and Great Society programs started to drain stockpiles of raw materials, including energy. Cars in 1968 went 120 miles an hour on four miles to the gallon of gasoline. Auto makers advertised their products by the size of the engine and horsepower.

The national attitude toward consumption began to erase initial benefits of inflation. As the seventies approached, inflation became a problem. Credit expansion and price appreciation started to accelerate, unaccompanied by real shifts in the economy. Instead, growth reflected shifts in investment. Performance stocks dominated the late sixties, followed three years later by the Nifty Fifty. Aronstein dates the start if the last gasp of the inflationary trend to about 1974, the year that the Organization of Petroleum Exporting Countries (OPEC) delivered a coup de grace in the form of an oil embargo. Sharp increases in oil prices goosed inflation. President Ford sallied forth with his *Whip Inflation Now* program. The government distributed millions of WIN buttons. But aside from employing workers in button factories, the effects were negligible, says Aronstein. As the price of everything from crude oil to Coca-Cola increased, inflation returned with a vengeance.

Cheap credit accommodated price expansion. The real interest rate—the difference between the rate of inflation and nominal interest rates—was very low in the seventies. At times it was negative, meaning that savings accounts lost money. "Savers were much, much too *credulous*," says Aronstein, using a favorite adjective. "After forty years of losing purchasing power, they finally got the message by 1979 that a host of changes had taken place."

Never dreaming that interest rates would go stratospheric before the seventies were finished, lenders began the decade by lending at long-term rates that were much too low. People invented new ways to pay for things they could not afford. Consumer credit exploded. Between 1970 and 1980 credit card receivables grew several-fold. Fifty years ago few people took out mortgages, which matured anyway in less than five years. So people did not buy houses that cost four times their incomes and pay them off over 30 years. That was a natural restraint on the price of residential real estate.

Rules changed once credit began to dominate the picture. Home buyers put down less and less cash. By the early eighties, lenders were accepting five percent down and lending customers the closing costs. It went largely unnoticed that money and credit were becoming interchangeable. "People weren't buying homes," says Aronstein. "They were buying mortgages." Instead of goods, people were buying credit to acquire the goods. The cost of the credit, not the price tag, determined affordability.

Nothing could beat letting individuals put down a tiny fraction of the purchase price for a house, the bedrock of American life. Ancillary to that were office buildings and shopping centers. America was becoming a gigantic real estate bazaar, rife with speculation. The accumulated credit worked itself to a point where it had to expand even more rapidly in order to keep what had gone before from imploding. And the door was open to using credit as anybody saw fit. Credit intended for building soon embraced less tangible activities, like taking over companies.

The trend just played into lenders' hands. After forty years of getting killed financially, they finally began to wise up. The first important step was aimed at stanching disintermediation, the flow of assets from banks to unregulated financial institutions. Deregulation of deposit rates made the banking system more fluid. Interest rates soared to nearly 20 percent, a major factor in the so-called "misery index" that helped defeat President Jimmy Carter's reelection bid in 1980.

Afterwards, lenders could apportion credit by price rather than strictly by availability. They could make credit too expensive for most people, but they could not make it unavailable.

There is a big difference. Too expensive requires judgment on someone's part. That was the problem through much of the eighties. The genesis of recent banking crises lay in the ability to borrow at almost any rate as long as borrowers could convince themselves and a banker that there was some chance of repayment.

The biggest new way to exploit credit availability was to boost the federal deficit. Despite the rhetoric of cost conscious, conservative presidents in the eighties, federal spending heaped coals on the fires of profligate borrowing, worsening the swollen credit burden. State and local governments also jumped into the borrowing business to an unprecedented extent, until states like Massachusetts and California started showing symptoms of severe indigestion. In mid-1992, California handed out IOU's to its employees in lieu of paychecks. Municipalities defaulted on debt obligations.

When loans pinned to crashing oil prices soured, serious faults appeared in the banking system. But instead of letting go when Texas banks were cooked and others were in deep trouble because of loans to oil-producing countries, especially in Latin America, the Feds added a turbo charger. The 1981 Tax Act, accompanied by enhanced deposit insurance, created, in effect, a Real Estate Speculation Act. It became almost unpatriotic for Americans not to speculate in commercial and residential real estate with federally insured deposits.

As if that wasn't bad enough, Wall Street discovered slick ways to disguise debt products of dubious credit quality that they were selling to eager consumers. A raft of hybrid instruments entered Wall Street's argot, terms like collateralized mortgage obligations (CMOs), collateralized bond obligations (CBOs) and real estate mortgage investment conduits (REMICs). The magic of diversification and federal guarantees transformed sows' ears into silk purses. Aronstein wrote Comstock's cocky broadside, *Snouts, Lips & Tails*, in February 1991.

> Of the many advances in the long history of commerce, the advent of sausage stands out as one of the greatest. The idea of taking something which, in pure form, would be repellent to potential customers, and by thorough grinding, mixing, reshaping and adulterating, creating an entirely new entity that could be marketed free from the taint of its original ingredients, marked a milestone in the annals of business thought.
>
> Sausage making is the prototype for an entire class of merchandising technique that has become particularly common in modern finance... The financial marketer who uses commingling as an approach is responding to the same general conditions that drive the sausage stuffer: an abundance of lower grade ingredients along with a hungry and credulous public.

Maybe hubris precipitated Comstock's rude shock in 1991. Or, perhaps, it resulted from obsessive fine tuning of a strategy that should have employed more flexibility. Fixed income strategies fizzled along with investments in sectors already flattened by the deflationary trend—commodities, precious metals and the like. Surveying the damage afterwards, the partners counted themselves lucky that they closed short positions in time. Had they been waiting to buy increasingly expensive shares to cover sales of shares they did not own, Comstock might have been forced to close its doors. But it was small compensation to be able to say that gloom had not completely run away with their senses.

Aronstein still wonders about the lapse that kept Comstock from going a bit further and buying stocks in time for the subsequent surge. He admits ambivalence. "I knew in my heart that we were making a mistake. I just thought it was going to be a small mistake." The answer may lie partly in Comstock's heady success as a bearish prognosticator. Hard-fought credibility rested on that position. "It had become too easy to just answer the queries and rattle off a story," he says. "It flowed too smoothly, and we didn't have to put up with so much ridicule [that] gets tiresome after a while."

This kind of situation is pervasive on Wall Street, says Aronstein. Pigeon-holing frequently thwarts investment managers who wish to break the mold they've cast for themselves. But when they try, investors get edgy. "[Investors] would like you to lay still and let them call you a growth manager or an asset allocater or an interest rate timer," Aronstein says. "And once you're successful, there is certain money that flows because of it. The system is just designed to channel money to people who make themselves easy to understand. You get the money because of the way in which people can categorize you," he says, "and secondarily because it was successful." It matters little whether the success relied on brilliance or plain luck. (Aronstein calls luck the "Jed Clampett effect," hearkening back to the most popular show on U.S. television in the mid-sixties, *The Beverly Hill Billies*. Jed Clampett was a hillbilly who discovered oil on his land while rabbit hunting, and moved his simple family to a mansion in Beverly Hills.)

There are countervailing arguments in favor of pigeon-holing. Investors often diversify by picking managers with different styles of management. The strategy runs aground if investment managers drift in unplanned directions. But Aronstein's point is that if maximizing returns is the chief objective, the system suffers from self-defeating restraints.

Causes aside, the blow to Comstock in 1991 shook Aronstein's rugged confidence for the first time. "This was the first big mistake," he says. "I've missed turns before or been on the wrong side of the market, but I've never been stubborn. Patience when you're on the wrong side of a trend is ruinous, and patience is a nice way of putting it."

Events did not cause the partners to abandon ship, however. Their contrarian strategy had weathered skepticism before, it just was never accompanied by such a sharp financial setback. In the final analysis, being too early is an endemic risk in their line of work, especially when forecasting economic upheavals that occur only once or twice in a century. "I don't know how to change it," Aronstein concedes. "Things that seem patently absurd to me, I assume other people can see. And I assume they are going to behave accordingly."

Concluding that their methodology was still intact left Minter, Salvigsen and Aronstein to mull a daunting puzzle: When would everyone else wake up to what was staring them in the face? "Sometimes things in here look so clear to us," Aronstein said at the time, "that we look out the window and say, 'Are we crazy? Are we looking at a different world?'"

Aronstein's literary hero, Wallace Stevens, may have asked himself a similar question while gazing out from the executive suite at the insurance company where he worked for much of his life. Like Aronstein, Harvard-educated Stevens straddled the worlds of finance and letters. While turning out poems at night, he spent his days working for Hartford Indemnity Company, a leading insurance company in those days. When he retired, Stevens was an executive vice president. "This guy is probably the finest poet of the century," says Aronstein. "And he was just leading purposely a sort of ordinary existence to the eye of anybody around him."

Sounding far more ethereal than is fashionable on Wall Street, Aronstein describes investment analysis as a crude but practical substitute for poetry and other loftier outlets for creative thinking. "Everything relates to the behavior of human beings in exchanging items of value," Aronstein declares. "So in that sense, poetry or philosophy is more vital than anything." It sounds outlandish, but plucking meaning from a few stanzas of blank verse may not be so different from interpreting an enigmatic series of economic events. After all, poetry and economics both have visible and invisible levels that don't always agree. Both call on intuition about forces shaping behavior and some sense of the past. Both exercise the mind's ability to render order from apparent randomness. Stevens's poem *The*

*Snow Man** reminds Aronstein that order exists even though it
is not easy to see.

> One must have a mind of winter
> To regard the frost and the boughs
> Of the pine-trees crusted with snow;
>
> And have been cold a long time
> To behold the junipers shagged with ice,
> The spruces rough in the distant glitter
>
> Of the January sun; and not to think
> Of any misery in the sound of the wind,
> In the sound of a few leaves,
>
> Which is the sound of the land
> Full of the same wind
> That is blowing in the same bare place
>
> For the listener, who listens in the snow,
> And, nothing himself, beholds
> Nothing that is not there and the nothing that is.

Inscrutable forces will decide ultimately whether Aronstein
is remembered as a gifted analyst or as misguided prophet of

---

* *The Snow Man,* by Wallace Stevens, from <u>The Palm at the End of The Mind</u>,
Vintage Books Edition, February 1990. Reprinted with permission of the
publisher.

doom. But as he guides West Course Capital along a contrarian path, Aronstein is sticking to his guns and his golf clubs. For him, that's the only rational choice in a world where most people fail to recognize what lies beneath the surface.

Chapter Four

*ALTHOUGH **DAVID L. BABSON** RETIRED FROM INVESTMENT MAN-agement in 1979, lessons from his exceptional career are still instructive. Invest for growth in sound companies and rewards will follow. Nay sayers be damned, says the blueblood contrarian who never gave a fig for the crowd's passing fancy. What seems obvious to everyone else, to Babson is suspect—as much today as in 1945 when Babson implored investors to buy fledgling companies like 3M, IBM and Union Carbide. The true story, meanwhile, is visible to those who patiently and conscientiously look for it. This successful philosophy spawned a family of mutual funds that now manages $1 billion under the highly respected banner of David L. Babson, Inc.*

David L. Babson

Don't Worry, Be Bullish

IT IS EASY TO IMAGINE THAT PROSPERITY SEEMED INEVITABLE TO anyone with an ounce of vision as World War II ended. A stream of innovations was about to transform the consumers' landscape, among them the first televised State of the Union message, and the first four-engine passenger airplane. "Films stake out claims to increase role in education at all levels...Baby Bathing and Economics Taught," ran the headline of a *Wall Street Journal* story. The President of Bell Aircraft, Lawrence D. Bell, told the New York Society of Securities Analysts that in ten years time helicopter manufacturing would surpass the business of building conventional, small aircraft.

On Broadway, "I Remember Mama" at the Music Box Theater and "Life With Father" at the Bijou celebrated a gentle past. A few blocks away, audiences experienced "The Glass Menagerie" by Tennessee Williams, a playwright whose searing work would redefine modern drama—if not modern America.

Yet Wall Street greeted January 1946 with jittery optimism. The world was at peace, at long last, but a four-year-old bull market was running out of steam after the longest advance since 1929. In fact, 1946 started poorly. Strikes or walkouts by nearly two million workers, and price ceilings held over from the war threatened to curtail production. Moreover, millions of returning servicemen revived fears of widespread unemployment. That threat prompted Secretary of Labor Henry Wallace, the former vice president and Socialist, to promote the Full Employment Act.

The nervous climate in early 1946 left a lasting impression on Robert Bleiberg, who joined *Barron's* that September (and later became its editor). "Everybody was persuaded that the prewar depression was going to resume," he recalls.

The prevailing view did not sit well, however, with David Leveau Babson. He made no secret of it. In weekly letters to clients of his fledgling investment firm, David L. Babson Co., he derided the so-called experts who warned investors to scurry for cover.

In the staid community of Boston's elite investment counselors like Scudder Stevens & Clark and Loomis Sayles, Babson's bullish advice was little short of a bombshell. He was no radical, no outsider, but a Harvard man and a Yankee with all the right credentials. Babson was one of their own. Yet there he was, urging a growing list of clients to sacrifice income and invest for growth—the very strategy that enjoyed a frantic heyday before the 1929 Crash propelled it into disrepute.

Tame sounding today, Babson's faith in the future looked to his depression-minded competitors like a prescription for disaster redux. It appeared to miss the paramount lesson of the Great Crash: preserve capital and invest for income.

Investors wanted returns they could put in the bank, not growth potential. On the strength of high dividends and yields, railroads and industrials like American Telephone & Telegraph found their way into nearly every stock portfolio. AT&T enjoyed exalted status after meeting every $9 dividend right through the depression. "It seemed almost every client who became a client owned AT&T," Babson says, his rich accent broadcasting Yankee heritage. To replenish capital paid out as dividends, however, AT&T had the habit of issuing new stock. So the dividends kept coming, but the stock price went nowhere.

Instead of investing for income, Babson & Co. proposed some mind-bending alternatives: Eastman Kodak, Dow Chemical, Minnesota Mining & Manufacturing, and Union Carbide—just a few of his recommendations that emerged from obscurity to become industrial powerhouses after World War II. Growing companies that emphasized research and reinvested a larger share of earnings, Babson argued, would never go out of style.

And as earning grew, so would the payout. Where others saw risk, Babson saw a lead pipe cinch.

That realization, and the willingness to act on it, set David L. Babson apart. "He was very much a pioneer," says Arthur L. Coburn, Jr., former chairman of the Trust Committee of the First National Bank of Boston, which he joined in 1925.

Yet singling out superlative investments like Eastman Kodak, 3M Corp., and IBM long before they became industrial giants seldom drew attention to Babson, a genial man with a quick, sometimes self-deprecating wit.

"My associates feel that as I fade away into the New Hampshire hills they will miss my stock market opinions more than anything else I've done for our firm," Babson wrote in the firm's June 1978 Staff Letter, the last one before he retired. "They say I'm their sure-fire bell-ringer—when Babson is bearish it's the sure-fire signal to buy—and vice versa."

Babson is also the man who blamed excesses of the late sixties on too many Freds—Fred Carr, Fred Mates and Fred Alger, three of the era's most celebrated go-go money managers. Usually, however, lavish praise went their way instead of to a man whose investment philosophy had stood the test of time for two decades.

"It always bothered us that our firm didn't seem to gain much recognition from this favorable record," he told members of the Newcomen Society in 1978, who were gathered to honor his remarkable career. "I think it was because we were considered 'contrarian' and never thought the conventional invest-

ment wisdom of the late forties and early fifties was very per-
ceptive—and we often said so publicly."

In those anxious post-war years, even short memories could
conjure up the 1930s, when fierce bear markets repeatedly
whipsawed investors who thought the worst was over. Each
time it looked as if the Dow had reached safe ground at last, the
floor opened up again.

The thirties were truly dismal for survivors of the Great
Crash, starting with three straight years of new lows for the
Dow, right on top of a horrendous 1929: down 34 percent in
1930, down 53 percent in 1931, and down still another 23 percent in 1932, to 59.93. Stocks leaped by two-thirds in 1933, to
99.9 then inched up in 1934 and 1935. In 1936 the Dow chalked
up a 58 percent gain, to 179.9, the biggest gain, percentage-
wise, in this century.

Then came 1937, a year many investors found more depressing than 1929. The market registered a post-crash high in February, then sputtered out of control for seven months after
President Roosevelt decided that the price of copper was too
high. By Labor Day, many safe stocks had lost half their value.
Investors headed for the hills.

The country's second largest investment advisor at the time,
Loomis Sayles, in Boston, urged clients to get out of stocks and
stay out. Most did, because Loomis did not become bullish
again on stocks until the middle fifties. Meanwhile, the investment field lost thousands of professionals and attracted few
new ones with fresh perspectives. "It was dismal in 1932, and
stayed dismal for twenty years," Babson recalls. "The invest-

ment business was a dead duck. We lost a whole investment generation, or maybe two." At one point he asked the Harvard Business School how many graduates went directly into the investment business. "There were virtually none in the late forties, zero."

After the debacle of 1937, preservation of capital reigned unchallenged for all but the most speculative accounts. Only huge dividends with long track records lured capital to common stocks—and few could meet that hurdle.

The Dow clawed its way up 28 percent in 1938, but the bear returned in 1939 and didn't budge until the Japanese drove General Douglas MacArthur from the Philippines in May 1942. From the peak in 1937 to the bottom in 1942, the Dow lost 41 percent. For the next three years, however, it matched the steady progress of Allied forces in Europe and the Pacific. (One notable exception taught Babson something about how markets discount expectation. Stock in Todd Shipyards slumped after December 6, 1941. Once war broke out, investors foresaw two alternatives: the US would either win the war or lose it. In either case, shipbuilding would slow down.)

On January 21, 1946, the *Wall Street Journal's* "Inquiring Investor" sounded this warning:

> It may go without saying that the investment
> portfolio which has been a highly desirable posses-
> sion under extraordinary conditions prevailing in re-
> cent years will require radical revision at some
> future time in order to conform to eventual changes
> in conditions: For investors of moderate means it
> will be particularly necessary to transfer funds into

prime quality, fixed income securities from common
stocks and sub-quality bonds...

More than 17 years after October 1929, most experts still advised mainstream investors to jettison common stocks when
uncertainty loomed. Babson, ever the stubborn Yankee, put his
fledgling company on the line by unfurling a contrarian pen-
nant. "Our point is that the popular viewpoint is often wrong,"
he wrote to clients in January 1946.

A staff letter in May laid out the evidence in typical fashion.
It measured a handful of fast-growing industries against the
Federal Reserve Board Index of Industrial Production, and
other business indices, to see how each had progressed between 1929 and 1944. The Fed Index had about doubled, but
growth companies' industrial activity far outpaced it. Chemi-
cals were up about 250 percent, soft drinks tripled and plastics
were up more than seven-fold.

In weekly letters, Babson described the future more clearly
than most investors can depict the past. But he was not the first
to champion growth companies. Who originated the growth
stock concept is a subject for unending conjecture, but some of
the credit must go to Edgar Lawrence Smith. His best selling
book, *Common Stocks as Long Term Investments*, turbocharged
demand for common stocks when it appeared in 1924. And
then there was the legendary tycoon John J. Raskob, whose
1929 article for the Ladies Home Journal must rank high in the
annals of ill-timed investment advice. Its seductive title:
"Everybody Ought to Be Rich."

Babson latched on to growth stocks around 1938, by accident, when shares of Minnesota Mining & Manufacturing came
to his attention through his wife's family. Like Babson, whose
ancestors settled in Gloucester, Massachusetts, in 1630, Katherine Allen descended from old Yankee stock. Her ancestors were
bankers in Salem, Massachusetts, who owned interests in clip-
per ships.

Perhaps growing up in a once-flourishing New England sea-
port nurtured Babson's contrarian nature. Sailing men and their
financial backers routinely flouted convention to expand commerce.

> Not only were the ports of Western Europe re-
> sorted to by a daily increasing number of American
> ships, but those of the Baltic and the Mediterranean
> were now for the first time visited by our country-
> men. Not content with this, our merchants turned
> their thoughts to China, to the Indian Archipelago,
> to the northwestern coast of our own continent, and
> the islands of the Pacific, several of which were dis-
> covered by our navigators. The courage and self re-
> liance with which these enterprises were
> undertaken, almost surpass belief.
>
> Merchants of Boston and Salem, of moderate for-
> tunes, engaged in branches of business which it was
> thought in Europe could only be safely carried on by
> great chartered companies, under the protection of
> government monopolies. Vessels of two or three
> hundred tons burden were sent out to circumnavi-
> gate the globe, under young shipmasters who had
> never crossed the Atlantic. The writer of this memoir
> knows an instance which occurred at the beginning
> of this century—and the individual concerned, a

wealthy and respected banker of Boston, is still living among us—in which a youth of nineteen commanded a ship on her voyage from Calcutta to
Boston, with nothing in the shape of a chart on
board but the small map of the world in Guthrie's
Geography.[1]

Long before Babson fell in love with and married the daugh-
ter of ship owners, he was enamored of sailing ships. He eventually wrote about Gloucester's early history for his senior
thesis at Harvard, winning him praise from the great historian
Samuel Eliot Morison—and a $150 prize, to boot.

Even now, Babson's modest three-bedroom home on a hill-
side in Millford, Hampshire, is decorated with paintings of sailing ships and sea captains, and filled with blue and white
oriental china that once served as ballast in the vessels Katherine's family bankrolled. Babson likes to point out one of his fa-
vorites: a ceramic urinal in the shape of a cat with a removable
head. There is also a captain's desk whose secret compartment,
when Babson discovered it, disclosed a sample of the first per-
forated postage stamp ever issued by the U.S. government.

Like their well-heeled peers, Katherine's family started investing in bricks and mortar when steam began to supplant sail
power. One of these investments was in the American Glue
Company, a supplier to Minnesota Mining & Manufacturing in
its infant days as a sandpaper maker. Starting in 1929, however,
the adhesives industry consolidated. Eventually the American

---

[1]This account is taken from <u>Lives of American Merchants</u>, by Freeman Hunt. A meticulous
observer of American business prior to the Civil War, Mr. Hunt wrote and published *Merchants' Magazine & Commercial Chronicle* from 1839 until 1858. The collection of profiles was
republished in 1969 by August M. Kelley, New York, New York.

Glue Company folded, leaving its shareholders little except the shares of 3M that it had acquired, probably in lieu of cash payments in earlier days.

As it turned out, shares of 3M were a far better find even than a rare stamp. In an era when some of the strongest companies in the U.S. were foundering, Babson stumbled on a tiny company whose earnings had grown almost tenfold from 1931 to 1938.

"That made a big impression on me," Babson says. "I said there must be other kinds of companies that do that, and I watched the record of Dow Chemical. It had done the same thing." So, too, it turned out, had companies like Eastman Kodak, IBM, and Union Carbide.

Other than passing the good word along to his wife's aunt, there was not a lot Babson could do at the time. He was employed by his father's second cousin, Roger Babson, the reputed Sage of Wellesley and the founder of Babson College.

Cousin Roger published Babson's Reports, a pre-eminent investment letter of that day, which later became part of Babson United. Young David, fresh from Harvard with a degree in history, did not exactly seem suited to give investment advice. "I was in this business at twenty and literally didn't know the difference between a stock and a bond," he says. But lack of experience didn't matter. Roger was looking for a protégé with the same last name, and jobs were scarce in those days, even for Harvard men.

Babson's father, who taught veterinary medicine at Harvard when city dwellers still owned horses, was also sending a second son to Harvard Medical School and another to Cornell Veterinary School. "It was time for somebody to get off of Dad's back," Babson says in his thick-as-heavy-fog Boston accent. The month in 1931 that he went to work for his famous cousin, the Dow touched 41, its lowest point of the century.

Before he learned much from Roger's rigorous statistical analysis, David Babson saw through the cousin who supposedly forecast the Crash. Not that it wasn't so, just that Roger had predicted the Crash regularly since 1926. "He did this every six months until September 1929," Babson says. "That was the peak, the Dow was at 380, and he made another prediction that we were going to have a great crash someday." Babson figures that a wire service reporter remembered the press release a few weeks later, took the remark for more than it was worth, and shipped the story out to every newspaper in the country.

Nevertheless, the newsletter lost subscribers, not least because Roger never bothered to warn them that a crash was imminent. "The first piece of work he sent me to do was to write to clients about a company called Automatic Merchandising," Babson says. "It was a coin machine company they had recommended [in 1929] at $30 a share. Some speculator or right minded fellow was offering an eighth per share, 12 cents for $30." But in 1931, Babson informed subscribers, an eighth was too good to refuse.

Babson began writing a syndicated newspaper column under Roger's name. The writing skills he picked up—Roger insisted on short words, short sentences, and short paragraphs—were invaluable when he started writing his own staff letter. So was his exposure to exhaustive business statistics that fed the investment letter.

But he learned also that giving advice in a general letter was not the way to handle investments for people and get the best results. "People wanted their advice related to personal circumstances," he says. At Babson's Reports we had tried a modified form of investment counsel and the response was enormous." But Roger quashed the idea. "He really didn't want to because if you are running a subscription service you run off another letter it doesn't cost anything except postage. [Personal counseling] required having a lot of people if you had a lot of clients and he wanted no part of that."

Using proceeds from his investments, Babson started his own firm. Roger was furious, but not because there was any real chance of passing the reins on to his young cousin.

"I wasn't there long when I found that he'd already had three presidents hired to take over when he retired. They had all disappeared, so I didn't think much about that," Babson says. "As a matter of fact I could visualize myself with him at eighty years old and him saying, 'David, what did you do that for?'" In fact, Roger lived well into his nineties, and to the end was still sending plays in from the bench.

The rationale for David's own firm was compelling at a time when all the established investment advisors were in lock step with each other. "Here was an opportunity, I thought, to do something and make my own mistakes and make our own mistakes with the other fellows," Babson says. "So that's the way we started it, and we worked like the devil." Such was the output that Babson apologized to his clients for skipping a staff letter the week of Christmas 1942.

Some old-fashioned marketing probably made Babson, at the start, the country's first discount investment advisor. "We knew what fees were being charged, so we started undercutting, because we couldn't see why you should pay these fees," he says. "We started out with a fee schedule that was quite different, and it was a great help to us [in getting established], but it didn't make a lot of money."

Besides Loomis and Scudder, there were two other investment counselors of any size at the time, one in San Francisco and the other, T. Rowe Price, in Baltimore. Like Babson, T. Rowe Price had developed a growth stock philosophy of his own, which he wrote about for *Barron's* in 1939.

Though Price and Babson met only once, and very briefly, their approaches could not have been more in synch. "We were about alike as two peas in a pod," says Charles W. Shaeffer, an original T. Rowe Price partner who eventually succeeded the founder as president. "Our ideas were so much alike you'd have thought we were in the same firm."

Competitors never bothered Babson, but Edson Smith did. Smith, the influential finance columnist for the *Boston Globe*, wrote *The Investor* in Babson & Co.'s formative days. "Every time I would read one of Edson Smith's daily columns I would get madder again," says Babson, whose anger still shows forty some odd years later. Smith frequently weighed in on the side of investment timing and dismissed the buy and hold approach as naive.

Gunning, evidently, for Babson in March 1946, Smith wrote:

> Some investment managers have so much confidence in their ability to pick out attractive individual situations and so little confidence in their ability to forecast the movement of the averages that they maintain a fully invested position all the time, concentrating their holdings in issues which they believe likely to be worth more eventually.
>
> Men who adopt this philosophy have found from sad experience that they are not the only ones who can figure values and that when they are waiting to buy a stock on weakness someone else probably is waiting to do the same thing.

Babson figured that comments like this one were aimed at him. "We were the only ones in the Boston community I know of who were taking an optimistic view," he says.

On July 1, 1946, the U.S. government phased out price controls. Fearing inflation and other destabilizing results, investors braced for the worst. They nearly got it four weeks later. On September 3, the stock market took its worst drubbing in nine years, tumbling 10.51 points in one day, or 5.6 percent, to 178.68.

"Opinions change rapidly on Wall Street," the Journal's "Heard on the Street" column noted on the morning after. "It was not so long ago that some technicians were predicting 250 or even 275 for the industrial average this year. Now, some of them are talking the possibility that the average may decline to 150 or even lower as the bear market progresses."

The swoon continued until September 19, when the Dow stood its ground just north of 165. All told, it had taken back a year's worth of gains, not good, but no rout either. A few weeks later Babson observed that the *New York Times* Business Index had just marked a peacetime high, and added a note skeptical of the persistent doomsday forecast. "Many investors fear that the country faces a severe depression in 1947. As one commentator aptly put it a few days ago, 'If we have a depression in 1947, it will be the best advertised one we have ever had.'"

No depression materialized in 1947, when both the economy and the stock market performed well. But the consensus remained guarded. There were constant comparisons to economic patterns following previous wars, especially World War I and the severe downturn three years after it ended.

Uncharacteristically, Babson vented doubts of his own in July 1947. Fretting over the precarious European economy, rising commodity prices, and a wage settlement with coal workers, Babson sounded like the pundits he usually railed against. "In short," he wrote, "we fear a renewal of the inflationary spiral will result in a DEpression rather than merely a REcession." But by December, he was his bullish self again, citing four positive economic trends: A more stable dollar, enormous pent-up demand for consumer goods, the introduction of labor-saving devices and cost-cutting machinery, and an end to declining wages.

In our opinion, the fundamental question today is NOT whether we will have a recession in 1948.

> Rather we believe the real question is: Is this the twi-
> light of U.S. capitalism or are we on the threshold of
> the greatest period of prosperity in our history?
> Bluntly, if you believe that this is the twilight of capi-
> talism, sell all your securities, (government bonds
> included), all your other property and buy a ticket to
> South Africa. If you do not think U.S. capitalism is
> licked, then keep your eye on the ball which is the
> next 10 years—not the next 10 days or the next 10
> weeks!
>
> Far from despairing over present day develop-
> ments (which included the possibility of conflict in
> Eastern Europe) we think investors should be look-
> ing forward optimistically—to the most prosperous
> decade they have ever known.

Population trends bolstered Babson's waxing confidence. Commuting between his home in Wellesley and Boston, Babson pored over census statistics and concluded that official predictions would fall short of the mark. To him, more people had to mean more houses, more schools, more hospitals and more services—more of just about everything business could produce.

In 1949 the country did suffer the well-advertised recession, but Babson kept right on promising a bright future. "I used to tell someone, if you buy stocks today you should be arrested for stealing," Babson says. Business muddled through the downturn. But far from collapsing, the Dow recrossed the 200 mark on December 30, an 18 percent gain for the year. That was the clearest sign yet that time had arrived to shake off the depression psychology. The growth stock era was dawning, as Babson's track record proved. By 1950, a $10,000 investment in ten growth stocks had risen 260 percent since 1940, while ten income stocks only increased their market value by about 15 percent.

Babson published his 1953 New Year resolutions in the staff letter:

- To pay no attention to my own or anyone else's guesses concerning what the 'stock market' is going to do over the next few weeks or months;
- To diversify my investments with the principal emphasis on those industries and companies whose expansion in sales volume and earning power over the years ahead appears inevitable based on all the facts now at hand;
- To think of myself as becoming a part owner of the business when I make an investment rather than merely buying a certificate that I hope I can sell to someone else at a higher price later on."

Vindication was not the end of the road for Babson, who became the industry's curmudgeon twenty years after sounding the call for growth stocks. "I think I've been a contrarian at two important stages in the last fifty years," Babson says. "In the late forties and early fifties when stocks were the cheapest statistically that they ever have been, cheaper than in 1932, and again in the late sixties, when they had what at the time was called the go-go period."

Instead of 20 percent in a year, the three Freds and other celebrated go-go money managers were shooting for returns far in

excess of 50 percent or even a doubling. They would goose returns by picking the right "performance stocks." But these companies were not the Eastman Kodaks or 3M Corps. of their day.
They sold cowboy boots and ice cream and soft drinks. Speculative frenzy, not underlying industrial might, drove their market value up. When it was working, some of Babson's clients
wanted those returns, too. But Babson stood his ground.
"When I think of the industrial might of America," he told an
audience, "somehow I don't think of Doctor Pepper."

Suddenly, though, the firm that advocated growth was cast
as a stick in the mud. "We did not get into aggressive growth
stocks," says H. Bradlee Perry, who succeeded Babson as chairman. "We were under a lot of pressure. It was not easy to say
that is not a good idea. It would have been much easier to go
with the flow." But Babson was resolute. In fact, he fired off a
blast at performance investing at the first conference of money
managers under the auspices of *Institutional Investor* magazine.
"Some associates here were concerned about such a strong
stand," Perry says. "But Dave did not waver at all."

Less than two years later, surviving go-go stocks were in the
cellar and Babson regained his laurels. In February 1970, *Institutional Investor* magazine celebrated this development with an
article entitled, "David Babson: A Triumph of Virtue in the
Long Run."

> As the gunslingers were shot down en masse at
> the corner of Broad and Wall over the past year, the
> few left to swagger into Oscar's to celebrate were
> some of the old boys who had almost been forgotten

in all the excitement of the past few years. Leading
them was David L. Babson, whose fund ranked fifth
in 1969 for U.S. funds with assets of over $10 million,
with a slight gain in a year when minuses prevailed.

Success eventually bred frustration, however. The Nifty Fifty phenomenon took hold of Babson's beloved growth stocks and swept their prices out of sight. In the drunken belief that this handful of companies would continue to grow and that demand for the stock would henceforth outstrip supply, investors bid prices up to gigantic price-earnings multiples.

"The most difficult time for the firm was when our approach became the fad," Perry says. "What had been contrarian became the popular thing to do. When growth stocks became overvalued, so much belief in long term approach forced us into under performance." When the Nifty Fifty re-entered the atmosphere, Babson & Co. got burned along with everyone else.

Crippled by multiple sclerosis, Babson retired at age 68 before big stocks rallied in the early eighties. At 82, Babson still tools around his New Hampshire home on a three-wheeled motor scooter. If he were starting all over in 1994, he says he would look for the same characteristics he looked for in 1943: companies with solid earnings credentials and long track records. He still rails against the main culprit, conventional thinking that almost always lures investors in crazy directions. "Things are obvious," he says, "if you just get away from running with the crowd."

Chapter Five

HUMPHREY NEILL, THE CELEBRATED SAGE OF SAXTON'S RIVER, Vermont, has inspired generations of contrarians. His advice to investors: Beware of the crowd, don't be swept up by euphoria or down by despair. When everyone thinks alike, watch out. They're probably wrong. Neill's sharp thinking and homespun aphorisms are no less appropriate today than when he began to formulate the theory of contrary opinion three quarters of a century ago. In fact, Neill's ideas formed the basis for the Contra Fund that Fidelity Management established in 1967 and still manages today.

Humphrey B. Neill

Vermont Ruminator

DEAR CONTRARIAN,

The stock market is always going lower (when it is headed down) and always is going higher (when it is headed up). Sounds stupid, doesn't it? but that about expresses the public psychology. The crowd rides the trends and never gets off until they're bumped off, so to speak. As I have ventured to say over and over again, "time and extent" are generally unpredictable, in economic swings. The market will stop going down when selling pressure is exhausted. That is all one can say with assurance, which isn't very helpful. Smart speculators buy their straw hats in January, they don't wait until the fourth of July. When the market breaks and pays little attention to why the advertised "climaxes" that is when contrarians look in their bank-books and negotiables and start to hunt around for values as they come into view.

Yours for sharp shooting through the fog and Wall Street,

Humphrey B. Neill.

This advice reached subscribers to the *Neill Letters of Contrary Opinion* in June 1962, about the half way point in the author's twenty-five-year crusade against conventional thinking. Every two weeks his Letters challenged readers to pierce the fog of public opinion by ruminating at length—Neill's primary activity at his farm in Saxton's River, Vermont.

To casual observers, Neill sounds eccentric. Not without reason. They see a curmudgeonly New England business writer spouting off on a topic only Wall Street's insiders are supposed to comprehend. Neill was an outsider. He dispensed advice to investors but left his own modest investments to the local bank. He talked about psychology just when experts were concocting efficient market theories and computerized investment strategies aimed at factoring out the human element.

Investors who knew the man *Life* magazine hailed in 1949 as the father of contrary opinion found in Neill one of the most colorful and clear-headed philosophers ever to mull the state of affairs on Wall Street. His disciples view contrary thinking as a compass for navigating any kind of market, especially when the going gets treacherous. His advice made many readers wealthier, and wiser too, according to their accounts. He articulated a consistent philosophy geared superbly for a fearfully volatile environment. Unlike so many shallow strategies that come and go with each peak or trough, Neill offered a theory with subtext ripe for reinterpretation, a wellspring for fresh ideas when hardest to come by.

True to his doubts about the crowd's ability to think in contrary manner, he never set out to convert a mass audience. Such an idea was anathema to him. His seminal book on the subject of contrary opinion has sold only 44,000 copies in 40 years. His newsletter, at peak circulation, had 2,000 subscribers. Neill relied on the masses for collective opinions, not for subscriptions.

He panned easy-money schemes and warned readers to temper enthusiasm whenever the crowd beckoned. He expressed a jaundiced view of charts when they were gaining popularity. "I have contended for years that when one needs guidance the most, charts help the least," he reminded an audience in 1969, just as computers appeared to herald a new age for stock analysis.

Shortly before Neill died, in June 1977, Fidelity Investments celebrated his exceptional career with an advertisement in the *Wall Street Journal*. It pictured Neill, still feisty at 82 years old, thumbs in lapels, speaking with a cartoon sketch of a Fidelity executive on the tenth anniversary of Contrafund, which had prospered by adhering to Neill's tenets. "Mr. Neill," said the Fidelity man, "I'd like to acknowledge your theories that led to the development of Contrafund. But tell us, sir, what have you been up to lately?"

Neill's reply was his trademark: "Ruminating, young man. Ruminating."

Not since the German philosopher Arthur Schopenhauer preached the virtues of idle contemplation has anyone attached so much importance to mere ruminating. Neill's prodigious ruminations produced *Tape Reading and Market Tactics*, in 1931, *The Art of Contrary Thinking*, in 1954 (and reprinted nine times) and *The Ruminator—A Collection of Thoughts and Suggestions on Contrary Thinking*, in 1975, as well as several other books on business topics. All this, in addition to the fortnightly *Letters*, which delivered contrary ruminations on business, finance and socio-economics until December 1974.

Albert Neill, Humphrey's son, still lives in the 18th century farmhouse where his father worked. Owned by Neill ancestors since 1828, the farmhouse sits on the edge of tiny Saxton's River, Vermont. Humphrey's exhortations left an imprint on his son. Al inherited his father's contrarian instinct, but he exercises it even farther from Wall Street. For months at a time in deprived parts of the world, he helps to set up food and health care programs.

He has been meticulous about keeping his father's writings and memorabilia. Humphrey's favorite books now fill the shelves of a handsome guest room, alongside field glasses and a message book that saw service in World War I. "He was always into things," Al says, wistful about his old man. "He always said how much better off I was than he was at my age," Al says. "But I'm not so sure. I think he had a pretty good formula."

Humphrey hammered away at his formula on a Royal typewriter in a room off the kitchen. In the barn, he kept a library crammed with dozens of volumes of historical statistics, business periodicals and other references. He did much of his ruminating in a nearby field behind the barn and across a stream.

"I am writing now in the shade of a hundred-and-twenty-five-year-old maple and can look through its massive branches to green pastures beyond," Neill wrote ten months after the Great Crash. "A delightful, century old house and neighborly barns somehow bring a quieting philosophy and a peaceful perspective upon the problems of Wall Street. One needs to get away frequently in order to realize that market fluctuations are not the all-important facts in life."

From this tranquil outpost, Neill challenged readers to break free of mental complacency. "The art of contrary thinking," he wrote in the foreword to the book with that title, "consists in training your mind to ruminate in directions opposite to general public opinions; and to weigh your conclusions in the light of current events and current manifestations of human behavior." He took his pen name, The Vermont Ruminator, from a favorite passage in Charles Dickens's *Pickwick Papers*, whose Mr. Pickwick indulged a fondness for "ruminating on the strange mutability of human affairs."

Neill emphasized again and again that thinking contrarily (to use the awkward term he coined) is no slapdash technique lending itself to mass appeal. "You have to absorb the idea," Neill said. "You cannot learn it, as you would learn the construction of an index, or would study chart formations. One has to let the idea soak in until unconsciously one becomes a contrary minded person who habitually considers the counter viewpoints on questions and problems as they arise."

In person, Neill was like his *Letters* —not exorbitantly charismatic or brilliant, but beguiling in a rustic, cantankerous, common-sensical way. "He was at the same time scholarly but also country, thoughtful without being antagonistic," says Eric Miller, a chief investment officer for Donaldson Lufkin Jenrette, the Wall Street investment firm. Ed Bragdon, who ran Fidelity's top-ranked Essex Fund for many years, found Neill charming, interesting, and "very quick and bright."

Edward C. "Ed" Johnson 2d, the man who built Fidelity Investments into a mutual fund powerhouse, personal finance maven Sylvia Porter, economist Elliott Janeway, were avid readers. So, too, were Edson Gould, the leading chart analyst of his day, and even the actor Marlon Brando. Dean LeBaron credits Neill with fostering an important turning point in his professional life, by validating the contrarian philosophy that has built Batterymarch Financial into a $12 billion pension management firm. Less celebrated members of the Neill fan club included Robert Smitley and Major L.L.B. Angas, two fascinating investors whose lives eventually intertwined with Neill's.

Ed Johnson instilled Neill's message in employees and, more importantly, in his own son and successor, Edward C. "Ned" 3d. "Although I cannot claim to be one of the first subscribers to your letter of contrary opinion," Ned wrote shortly after Neill retired, "back in 1955 when I was stationed in Germany, your letter of contrary opinion was the one piece of written material my father chose to send me hoping maybe that I might be properly indoctrinated in the best methods of making money in the stock market. You deserve a great deal of credit for having developed this approach to investment which I am sure you are aware have applications in many parts of one's life."

Sylvia Porter paid homage this way: "Humphrey Neill is far more than a colorful, white-thatched almost 75-year-old Vermonter who has commanded the attention of professional economists for three decades by defying conventional economic theories," she declared in a 1969 newspaper column. "He is a serious-minded free thinker whose Contrary Opinion Theory has earned mounting respect in economic circles across the land."

John Train, an investment manager and author of several best-selling books on finance, including *The Money Masters*, penned this inscription in his first book, *Dance of the Money Bees*: "For Humphrey Neill, the wisest of all financial writers and philosophers, from a devoted friend of many, many years."

Neill's call to contrary thinking snared actor Marlon Brando, when he was looking for ways to manage his newfound wealth. "Since writing you last I have become infected, shall I say, with gold fever to the point where we are about to open a most promising property," Brando wrote in June 1961. "We can do very nicely with gold at $35 an ounce, but we would be strained if gold were worth say $18. Do you see anything in the future which would influence the price of gold down or up?... When you have a moment between your most instructive and enjoyable letters, I'd like to have your horseback opinion on the future of gold as such."

Neill replied to Brando in typical fashion—self effacing but colorful and well-informed: "You'll agree that a horseback opinion may come a cropper five minutes after the rider mounts the horse. He then feels like a jackass, I'm afraid!"

> In the present era, it seems very doubtful to me that gold will have increased usage in either private or government transactions. The powers-that-be are likely to tie themselves to gold: they do not desire the "discipline of the gold standard" we hear so much about from the gold adherents... However, that has nothing to with selling gold at $35 an ounce... I see nothing in the future that will put the price of gold down - but there is obviously the possibility of a future panic that will put it up.

In a grateful letter dated July 17, Brando announced that he had optioned a new property in partnership with mining expert Richard Phalen, nephew of a former U.S. senator from California.

The widely syndicated columnist Roger Babson, better known than Brando for investment savvy, also held Neill in high esteem. One of Babson's newspaper columns carried this advice: "A popular stock of the day is not a good inflation hedge. For reasons, write my friend Humphrey Neill, the Great Contrarian of Saxton's River, Vermont." Only encroaching blindness, at 91 years old, stopped Babson from reading Neill's letters, according to Babson's assistant.

Neill roused critics, too. But far from blunting their barbs, Neill often welcomed them as grist for his own subsequent contrary opinions. "The angrier he got the more he wanted to hear what you had to say," says economist and author Peter L. Bernstein. Following a difference of opinion about where government spending was needed in the sixties, Neill invited Bernstein to speak at a contrarian forum. He spoke at several more afterwards.

Critics targeted Neill unfairly over the issue of market timing. Frenzies feed on frenzies, gloom begets more gloom. Recognizing prevalence of despair or gloom does not pinpoint when investors will regain their senses.

Neill agreed. *The Art of Contrary Thinking* stated categorically that short term market timing was never his intention. "If one relies on the Theory of Contrary Opinion for accurate timing of his decisions he frequently will be disappointed." Also, "...It is more of an antidote to general forecasting than a system for forecasting. In a word, it is a thinking tool, not a crystal ball." Far from intending contrary theory as a means of market timing, Neill had a sensible antidote in mind. "Inasmuch as it is next to impossible to accurately time the reactions of the crowd, it is advantageous to consider the opposite of what appears probable. The crowd has been wrong so frequently in their opinions, especially in timing, that it is imperative to look on the unsuspected side of all questions and all predictions."*

His first stock market book, *Tape Reading and Market Tactics*, illuminated the purpose Neill did have in mind. It was also a

---

* This and other excerpts from *The Art of Contrary Thinking* and *The Ruminator* printed with the kind permission of Caxton Printers, Caldwell, Idaho.

success that is still in print. "The question when to act contrary
to the public, is a difficult one to answer," he wrote. "At important *turning points*, I believe it is safe to state, the public is *always* wrong—that is, the majority... I adopted this theory in
November, 1930, to detect the temporary bottom of the long decline. The public wanted to go short at the bottom. Prices had
sagged for so long a period that it was finally considered that
short sales were the only way to make money. However, when
everyone wants to buy, or when everyone wants to sell, look
out!"

Neill's take on his elusive theory began to crystallize in the
late 1920s, according to an uncompleted autobiography.

> As closely as I can calculate, I became imbued
> with the spirit and practicality of 'contrary opinions'
> in 1929. It was a wildly fluctuating time in the stock
> market all year, climaxed as everyone knows by a
> smashing end of America's most expansive decade.
>   It was not unnatural, I suppose, that with my in-
> quiring and advertising type of mind, I stood aloof
> from, yet was closely drawn to, the trading activity
> in stocks.

Neill discovered his "advertising type of mind" by accident.
He was born in 1891, the son of Albert Barnes Neill and Carrie
Elizabeth Bancroft. He and a sister grew up in Buffalo, New
York, where their father, Albert Barnes Neill, managed a
foundry that manufactured iron wheels for locomotives. His
parents also represented the union of two families that owned

Buffalo's leading department store, Barnes, Bancroft & Co. As a restless thinker, Neill found mostly tedium in school. A stint at prep school was disastrous. "A black spot," Neill called it. Although an ancestor was one of the founders of Amherst, Neill forewent a sure college acceptance to join the U.S. Army, under the command of General John "Blackjack" Pershing.

He soon saw action, in pursuit of the Mexican revolutionary Pancho Villa. Later, When Pershing led the American Expeditionary Force into World War I, Neill held the rank of lieutenant and fought again. The Great War's conclusion hastened the start of Neill's professional career. He became an instructor in the army school of salesmanship, a program aimed at acclimating doughboys to peacetime careers.

On returning to Buffalo, he landed a job with a company that supplied display material to merchants. But it soon foundered. Married by then, Neill went on the road, hawking sun lamps to doctors in Kentucky, West Virginia and Tennessee. The economic slump in 1921 put an end to that business, too. Next he found his way to Orange, New Jersey, where, at last, he fell into a niche he liked, writing advertising copy for local companies. It was a scanty living, though. So to drum up a full-time job, he invented "The Writer Man," a tongue-in-cheek newsletter that he sent to prospective employers. This item was typical:

AN EXPERT

A friend handed me the following clipping. I regret that I can't quote the source of such a delicious yarn. It seems that a seaboard bank published this classified ad:

Wanted—A clerk. Must be experienced in foreign exchange. Salary, $10 a week.

And this is one of the replies received:

Dear Bank—I would respectfully apply for the position you offer. I am an expert in foreign exchange, in all branches. In addition, I converse fluently in Gum Arabic, Gorgonzola, Zola and Billingsgate. I write shorthand, longhand, left hand and right hand. I can supply my own typewriter if necessary, and I may mention that I typewrite half an hour in ten minutes, the record. I would be willing also to let you have the service, gratis, of my large family of boys, and if agreeable to you, my wife would be pleased to clean your office regularly without extra charge. The cost of postage for your answer to this application can be deducted from my salary. Please note that if you have a back yard, I would make bricks in my spare time.

Awaiting your reply, I remain...,

I, too, am willing to bring along my Corona, but my youngsters are too small to work and my wife is kept busy cleaning up after my pipes.

The biggest printer in New York hired him and assigned him to a client in the shoe manufacturing business. Soon Neill had a hard-bound book to his name: *Building A Profitable Retail Shoe Business.* He moved up next to sales and advertising manager for an ice cream company located on Long Island. Then, in 1928, he found his way to Wall Street, just as that era's stock market frenzy was racing to a climax. He became vice president and promotion manager for Wetsel Market Bureau. This was a subsidiary of Brookmire Economic Service, then a leading stock market advisory service.

Fifty years later, the *Journal of Portfolio Management* asked him to reflect on the Great Crash. "Strangely, commuting daily to work and visiting around the city, there was the most extraordinary acceptance of what happened in October 1929 (and in November, when the final disgorging of margined shares took place). People were sobered, of course, but it became the fashion to make a joke of it all.

Vaudevillians staged their acts around the crash, and fired joke upon joke at Wall Street, always getting their laugh. (One is still repeated, about the room clerk who wanted to know, 'Does the gentleman wish a room for sleeping or jumping?') Eddie Cantor wrote a little book, *Caught Short*, which sold on every newsstand."

After the crash, he convinced Wetsel to publish *If, As and When*, a booklet of "Passing Thoughts and Reflections on Human Nature in Finance." Writing under the pen name, The Market Philosopher, Neill found his contrarian voice. "It does little good to leave Wall Street for summer resorts where stock tickers and business gossip continue," he wrote in July 1930. "If you do go away, get beyond the fringe of advertising billboards and chambers of commerce. Seek the woods and hills; visit the villages where bread and butter is earned by the sweat of the brow and where, in the evenings and on Sunday, you join in good fellowship with your neighbors instead of in worship of the Almighty Dollars."

A new Neill persona surfaced as the Market Cynic, the pseudonymous author of *Ten Ways to Lose Money on Wall Street*:

1. Put your trust in board-room gossip.
2. Believe everything you hear, especially tips.
3. If you don't know, guess.
4. Follow the public.
5. Be impatient.
6. Greedily hang on for the top eighth.
7. Trade on thin margins.
8. Hold to your opinion, right or wrong.
9. Never stay out of the market.
10. Accept small profits and large losses.

When Brookmire sold Wetsel in 1931 to raise cash, Neill and a colleague, Buck Tyson, formed their own service, Neill-Tyson Inc. In addition to advising individual clients, Neill-Tyson supplied twenty stock averages along with daily commentary to two newspapers, the *New York World Telegram* and the *Christian Science Monitor*. But 1931 also brought a more meaningful development, the publication of Neill's first major foray into financial journalism, *Tape Reading and Market Tactics*. In a rare reference to the results of his own investments, Neill dedicated the book to losses he had suffered, "With a deep appreciation for the experience and knowledge each loss has brought me."

Tape Reading cut through popular mystique and described in lay terms just how the ticker tape reveals strategies used by professional speculators. Many caveats are still valid today, not least a warning that playing the market for hourly or daily fluctuations amounts to "a risky, foolhardy enterprise." The book also articulated Neill's fix on a human dimension seldom associated with tape reading.

> The ticker tape is simply a record of human nature passing in review. It is a record giving us the opinions and hopes of thousands of people. We must dismiss from our minds all other facts. Precious few know, or can hope to know, who is buying or selling. We hear that So-and-So is buying; he may also be selling, through another broker. If he wants us to know that he is buying, we should be chary. So, let us disregard hunches and wild conjectures. If he buys and sells, the record of his transactions will be on the tape. We must make our interpretation from the record. So long as we continue to guess who is doing the buying and selling, we shall remain in a sea of confusion.

In the 1930s, Neill's career took almost as many turns as the volatile stock market. Neill-Tyson lasted only a short time before Tyson went his own way. Neill kept the business going briefly, then liquidated it and returned to Brookmire, which was trying to stage a comeback. Brookmire published Neill's second hardback book, *Investment Management and Portfolio Control*, a call for intelligent portfolio diversification.

When Brookmire's fortunes slid lower still, Neill lit out on his own to write business books. He also tested the idea for a letter of contrary opinion. "I believe the initial idea of a 'letter of contrary opinions' came to me in 1936 or 1937," he later wrote, "when the stock market went through gyrations that had everybody, including the experts, scratching their heads to learn what happened. (The drop in prices in 1937 was the swiftest ever recorded)." The newsletter's casual format may have drawn inspiration from a friend, mentor and stalwart contrarian, Robert L. Smitley, who published (whenever it suited him) a newsletter of his own, *Occasionally from RLS*.

After graduation from Yale in 1904, Smitley headed for Wall Street. He started out as a runner, hustling checks and securities around the financial district. Shrewd investments parlayed $1,000 in seed money into a seat on the New York Stock Exchange by 1907—which carried an $81,000 price tag in those days. But according to Neill, in a foreword to one of Smitley's books, Smitley soon tired of the brokerage business, and left it to edit a weekly newspaper. Then came a stint as business manager for the *Magazine of Wall Street*, a Hearst publication, before he could indulge a deeper interest in books.

Smitley yearned to start a business book shop. Opportunity presented itself in November 1918. In an unpublished memoir, Smitley described how the world-famous Dixie Business Book Shop was born—in exemplary contrarian fashion.

> The logical basis for such a Shop had already been established by Colonel Eugene Levy though he had little knowledge of the subject and less interest. Many of us often dropped in to see the Colonel - he fought bravely in the Confederate Army - and listened to tales of war and the South. Very little of the noon hour period was devoted to economics or books on business.
> On the false armistice day in November 1918, when nearly everyone attempted to drink up the available supply of champagne and sparkling bur-

gundy, I dodged out of the furor and escaped from the milling mob. I recall going down the steps of 41 Liberty Street and seeing the old Colonel seated at his desk, almost asleep. My method of approach to the buying of his establishment would not have met with the approval of capable businessmen. The idea of this shop was a hobby and I hadn't the slightest idea that it would ever do more than pay expenses. In fact it might become a costly habit. My own family and many friends considered me definitely non-compos. I probably just escaped commitment in a state hospital. But the desire to get away from "big business" and do something I really wanted to do overcame all business sanity. And I knew the Colonel had an immense stock of business books.

Anyhow, there was the Colonel. My approach awakened him from his nap. As soon as I could get my breath I said, "You want to sell this Shop?"

"Yes," replied the Colonel.

"How much?"

"Fifteen hundred dollars," replied our Southern gentleman.

"You've sold it," I said.

Due diligence elicited only one fact from the Colonel, that gross proceeds came to about $25 a day. Otherwise, Smitley was on his own. The shop flourished along with the economy in the 1920s, as legendary investors Jesse Livermore and Bernard Baruch browsed alongside their would-be imitators. In 1933, Smitley published a book of his own, *Popular Financial Delusions*.

Smitley became known as the world's leading authority on business and economic literature. Harvard's Baker Library, other leading libraries and a handful of wealthy individuals enlisted his help in filling bookshelves devoted to business and economics. But as the depression deepened, interest in business books flagged. Slowed, too, by illness and several serious operations, Smitley closed Dixie's doors in 1942.

Between 1937 and 1940, Neill turned out three books of his own: *The Untold Stories of American Business*, *Understanding American Business* and *48 Million Horses*. Except that industrial might was an out of favor topic as the depression approached its tenth year, none of the books especially reflected Neill's contrarian bearings. That could be why none enjoyed as warm a reception as *Tape Reading*.

Untold Stories was cast as "an inspirational book for business executives," full of stories portraying business in its most romantic light. Concerned that students were largely ignorant about business, Neill produced *Understanding American Business*, a high school textbook produced in conjunction with the National Better Business Bureau and marketed by Macmillan & Co., the leader in textbook publishing in those days, schools didn't buy it. Though it was eventually published by J.B. Lippincott in Philadelphia, the original idea for *48 Million Horses* came from the Kingsport Press, a business book publisher that envisioned a series of books promoting business. The first candidate, American Can Company, turned Neill down on the advice of its legal department, which saw no value in exposing the company to limelight. So Neill approached General Electric, where he knew Phil Reed, assistant to the president.

Reed secured approval for a book that became a cloying paean to the electrical power industry. "It may as well be stated at the very beginning that this book glorifies success. While failure is more dramatic than success and disaster more gripping than smooth sailing," Neill wrote in the foreword, touching on a theme he would revisit later in a contrarian context, "yet, in America, there is an innate admiration for the job well done. And today, jobs are being well done with electric power."

An unexpected connection enabled him to start research for a book about the New York Stock Exchange. Brushed off by the Big Board's public relations man, Neill arranged to present his idea to the public relations committee, he told an interviewer from *Vermont Business World*. Learning that Neill was the nephew of an Amherst professor by the same name was enough to satisfy the committee chairman. "Gentlemen," he said, "this man's uncle was my favorite college professor and he looks like a good enough man. I suggest we go ahead with whatever he wants."

Drumming up a publisher was trickier. Although publishers flock to scandals these days, scandalous developments on Wall Street once made them nervous. The first publisher, Kingsport Press, got cold feet when news surfaced that Richard Whitney had been caught stealing from investors. Whitney was no lightweight. He was a former president of the New York Stock Exchange and brother of the man who ran powerful J.P. Morgan & Co. "You can't imagine the shock," Neill told a reporter years later. "It was obvious I wasn't going to talk to anyone about that book on that day." In fact, ten years passed before B.C. Forbes published the book.

By summer 1941, Neill was getting ready to move his family from the New York suburb of Larchmont to Saxton's River. His son, Albert, remembers no discussion. "My father said we were giving Larchmont back to the Indians," Al says. And that was that.

In preparation for the migration north to the ancestral home, Neill bought a local business, the Hildebrand Animal Photographic Service. He was an avid photographer who entered competitions, but he never pursued photography as more than a "commercialized hobby" that would cover expenses. He was an experienced photographer, but he never pursued the Hildebrand business aggressively. During World War II he used his limited gas rations to travel around selling war bonds. He also continued to write regular columns for *Financial World* and for the *Christian Science Monitor*. Meanwhile, he signed on with the volunteer fire department and tried small-time farming by raising a handful of horses, goats, cows and a few hundred chickens.

A few weeks after settling in Vermont, Neill decided to stop writing his occasional Letters of Contrary Opinion. "Well, it looks as if this would have to be your contrary-writer's l'envoi. A few enthusiastic souls have written, asking that these Contrary Letters be kept alive, but the large majority of readers apparently agree with me that, having formed the habit of thinking contrarily, there is no pressing reason for these Letters."

Sniffing a bleak consensus in early 1942, he wrote "Harvest Time Ahead for Contrary Thinkers," for *Financial World*. "From this writer's contrary calculations, we are now in the midst of one of these periodic over-swings. The Ides of March," he wrote guardedly, "will (approximately) date another juncture when those who have the nerve to "cross" the gloomy public, pessimistic Wall Street and bearish forecasters, will have the pleasure (some time hence) of turning *profitably pessimistic* when present-day bears become optimistic bulls." A month later the market scraped bottom, followed by a bull tear that did not falter until September 1946.

He also interrupted self-imposed retirement from newsletters with intermittent letters to a few friends. In August 1946, "Theories & Queries from a Vermont Farmer-Writer" rambled on about politics. It mainly revealed his extreme conservatism (he called himself a "realistic reactionary") and deep satisfaction with the decision to leave New York. "Having lived year-round in Vermont, on a small farm for five years, I know that nothing can drag me back to the city."

A pronouncement during bearish 1947 proved so prescient that Neill's friend and disciple Garfield Drew reprinted it in a popular book, *New Methods for Profit in the Stock Market*:

> As stock prices have grudgingly given way, opinions have increased rapidly on the 'bear' side, until today there is no question in the Ruminator's mind but that the general opinion about the near-term future of the stock market is decidedly of one mind: Down.

> Inasmuch as this writer never recalls a time when
> the opinions of both professional forecasters and the
> public have been right when they have been in
> agreement, this would appear to be another instance
> where it would be unwise to join mass opinion and
> expect immediate lower prices and a continuation of
> the bear market.

Over the next two months the market climbed from its lowest level to its peak for 1947. *Life* picked up his comments again in the March 1949 article that catapulted him into the public eye. A story about investing called Neill "a sharp-eyed Wall Street trader" with a fine solution for a puzzling stock market: the theory of Contrary Opinion. A photo of Neill, in his beloved hunting shirt, took up twice as much space as photos of legendary financiers John J. Raskob and Bernard Baruch.

Even in the wake of notoriety, Neill never took all the credit for the theory of contrary opinion. "The contrary-opinion idea is not new," Neill wrote. He cited a number of precursors, including this observation by the 19th Century economist and logician William Stanley Jevons: "In making investments it is foolish to do just what other people are doing, because there are almost sure to be too many people doing the same thing." Neill filled his contrary-minded books and letters with evidence of his exhaustive reading—citations from literature, philosophy, history and economics with any bearing on the study of crowd psychology.

Life prodded Neill back into action. He hired a business manager and relaunched his C.O. letters the following November.

Sudden notoriety also encouraged B.C. Forbes to publish, after a ten year hiatus, *The Inside Story of the Stock Exchange*. Publication was filled with promise. Malcolm Forbes hosted a luncheon at 21 Club and important people supplied dust jacket testimonials. "Neill is a shrewd analyst of trends and an attractive writer," said Herbert Elliston, editor of the Washington Post. Neill's pal Philip Reed, by then chairman of General Electric, also offered praise. Raymond Villers, a noted authority on business and a faculty member at Columbia University, offered this: "He has the rather rare ability of writing upon financial subjects in a style that is human and entertaining—yet is not weakened by oversimplification. His story of the [New York] Stock Exchange should be a welcome addition to Wall Street literature and prove popular not only with the general reader, but also with younger students who are today pondering the question, 'Why a Wall Street?'"

Unfortunately, a slightly different question decided the book's fate: "Why a book about Wall Street?" Readers at the time were not yet obsessed with money men and the inner workings of a complex financial institution. A disappointed Neill blamed lackluster sales on Exchange directors who expressed displeasure with the critical appraisal of their performance as overseers.

The success of his rejuvenated Letters of Contrary Opinion softened the blow. Neill threw himself into the fortnightly undertaking, and thereafter stuck to writing exclusively about contrary opinion. In 1954, the Caxton Printers of Caldwell, Idaho, published *The Art of Contrary Thinking*. It is, by any standards, an odd book. For 200 pages, Neill exhorts readers to get out of their rut with theories, anecdotes, analogies, caveats and aphorisms.

Section One (It Pays To Be Contrary) lays out the foundation for contrary thinking. "I turned to a study of mass psychology in the hope of finding the answer to the riddle of 'why the public is so often wrong' (and that meant why I was so often wrong)," he wrote. "I dug into old books on the manias of speculation; I read everything I could get my hands on that pertained to the actions of crowds." In addition to his own observation that crowds seem prone to error, he discovered *Extraordinary Popular Delusions and The Madness of Crowds*, Charles Mackay's 1841 account of several centuries of investment schemes and manias all springing from the perennial human weakness for doing what others are doing.

The book's longer second section comprises "Essays Pertaining to the Theory of Contrary Opinion and The Art of Contrary Thinking." Chapter headings sound like a weird cross between Lewis Carroll and Milton Friedman: "On Predicting the Unpredictable," "Looking Two Ways at Once," "Thinking in Circles," "A Think-It-Out-For-Yourself Kit," "A Fallacy in Economic Extrapolation," "Read-and-Needle is the Contrary Way," "Limbering Up Your Mind," and "Capitalism's Basic Factor: Earning Power," to name a few of more than seventy separate headings. "Why Forecasts Go Haywire" is typical:

> Making predictions has become a mania. Practically all economists are called upon for their future views—and many go out of their way to write arti-

cles and make speeches about "what's ahead." You hear all manner of theories proposed and presented.

But the significant fact for us to hold before us is that the more prominence predictions receive the more inaccurate they are likely to be.

...We have seen the science of forecasting pass through various stages as this or that theory has come into the spotlight. Remember how Lord Keynes and Keynesianism were most talked about only a short time back? Today there seems to be a leaning toward mathematics and slide rules, the factors being analyzed in an engineering manner. And so it goes: everyone constantly hunting for the key to the future.

However, it would appear that composite predictions by authoritative forecasters can never prove out because their acceptance will be their downfall.

If you believe the predictions, you act against them to protect yourself. Thus, you help the predictions to go haywire.

I think I am on safe ground in asserting that so long as predictions remain popular, and are so numerous as they are today—and so long as they receive notoriety through repetition in the press and on the radio—*contrary opinions will increase in importance as thinking aids.*

He indulged to excess an advertising man's weakness for catchy slogans. "When everyone thinks alike, everyone is likely to be wrong," was a favorite. Sometimes, the absence of a consensus is a tip-off: "When everyone ignores a vital subject, it is likely to be important to everybody," Frequent uniformity in the media prompted this observation: "When writers write alike, readers think alike."

While Neill was still basking in *Life's* afterglow, his friend Major Lawrence Lee Bazley Angas came to live in Saxton's River. That Neill encouraged the Major to make the move is an awesome tribute to the depth of Neill's contrarian nature. The two men were polar opposites. Neill was quiet, thoughtful, modest and content with relative obscurity. Major Angas— British émigré, financial adviser and egregious self-promoter— became the flamboyant toast of Wall Street in the years surrounding the outbreak of World War II. His story is worth telling in part because of how it intertwined with Neill's, and also because he exemplified a prevailing mood on Wall Street that Neill rebelled against.

"The Major," as Angas was known, held court at the Waldorf Astoria, charging vast amounts for investment advice. "Sticking your neck out is always jolly. I like to be right gloriously or wrong gloriously," he told interviewer Earl Wilson for a *Saturday Evening Post* story in July 1940. Of some 5,000 financial advisors plying their perilous trade during the depression, none was more richly compensated than Angas, according to Wilson. "Only one investment counsel has ever topped Major Angas' $100-an-hour consultation fee: Major Angas. The Major used to charge $200. He announced the $100 fee as a sort of bargain special." His clients, cut rate or otherwise, included J.P. Morgan and the United States Treasury. At $500 a pop, the Major gladly held forth on topics ranging from stock market gyrations to the dire threat posed by communism to the Major's favorite activity—golf.

In the decades before or since the Major disembarked on U.S. shores, Wall Street has seldom seen anyone like this great grandson of George Fife Angas, founder of the National Bank of London. "Scion of one of England's glossiest banking families, Angas is a stock market prophet for the sheer hell of it," Wilson wrote. "Do it with dash is his way of life. Where most counsels prefer to whisper their forecasts, he shouts his. Because most counsels get distressed about pamphlet-writing forecasters, he has written fifty pamphlets and is always composing a fresh one. When Wall Street calls him "Major Anguish"—as it does after he makes a wild prediction—he may reply with a prophesy twice as breath-catching."

Two brilliant pronouncements brought him fame in the United States. Both were contrarian in nature. In 1926, after exhaustive examinations of every industry, the Major predicted a rubber market crash—a far more significant development in days before plastics. He foresaw that excessive international restraints on rubber could not last, and that expanded output would lower prices, turning boom to bust. His pamphlet, "The Coming Collapse in Rubber," drew jeers at first—until it materialized a few months later. Eight years later, Max Schuster, of Simon & Schuster, recalled another Angas pamphlet, "The Coming English Boom." Schuster envisioned an American version, and Angas complied. They published "The Coming American Boom" in July 1934, "on a Monday when the market was so dull that brokers and customers' men were playing bridge and pitching quarters. Trading was dragging down to 275,000 shares—the lowest in ten years," the *Post* reported.

> But over in the brokerage house of J.S. Bache and Company, something was happening. The company was giving away 2500 copies of the Angas book to customers and employees. Before night, the Street was reading and talking. On Tuesday, trading shot up to 579,000; on Wednesday, it boomed to 1,295,710. Prices climbed.

The predicted boom did not arrive overnight, however. Major Angas said that Americans mistook him. "I forecast a boom," he said, "I did not forecast a boom in July." Besides, he used boom to mean the rising half of a business cycle—not, as Americans supposed, to mean "a wild wave of continuous activity in the stock market." In any event, *Fortune* magazine observed in 1937 (the year the Big Board suffered its worst drubbing ever) that Major Angas "possessed a reputation for being infallible for ten years." That period saw the publication of one pamphlet after another, holding forth on subjects as different as *Investment for Appreciation, The Inarticulate Republicans and the Vote Buying Democrats*, and the *ABC of Socialism*.

When precisely Angas met Neill is uncertain, but they crossed paths because Brookmire engaged Angas as a consultant. One story has it that their first meeting took place at the Major's plush bedside, where he often received interviewers in regal fashion. The lure of high living eventually wore off on the Major, or wore him down, because around 1950, at Neill's urging, he relocated to tiny, sleepy Saxton's River. He grew up in the English countryside and wanted to return to it, according to Joan "Bunny" Pulver, the secretary who worked for him in New York and accompanied him to Vermont. (Angas started calling her "Bunny" after she showed up once with ear muffs that looked like rabbit ears, and the moniker stuck.) After sharing office space in one of the town's two commercial buildings. he bought the local hotel and took up residence there, filling rooms, floor to ceiling, with his voluminous library. Convinced that papers stored vertically stuck together and became lost, the Major would not tolerate filing cabinets.

Angas took to his bucolic surroundings faster than puzzled local folks took to his peculiar ways. Humphrey's grandson, David Neill, remembers Angas as "the most eccentric, out of place person in this village." Stories abound: the Major, in his pajamas, chipping golf balls all night on his front lawn, ice skating with pillow tied around his waist, maintaining six Cadillacs with loving care, or drying his socks on the radiator of the local movie theater, during a show. He would ask acquaintances to walk on his back to relieve pain still caused by a World War I bullet lodged near his spine. He disliked uninvited visitors. Seeking contributions for the local girl scouts, Blanche Sheehan left Angas with a generous $10 donation—after promising never to return. Halloween horrified the Major.

All the while, Angas turned out his advisory newsletters, which frequently crusaded for a return to the gold standard in the unrelenting expectation that dark days lay ahead. One investor asked his father-in-law why he subscribed to a newsletter that was wrong 100 percent of the time. Because, said his father-in-law, whenever exuberance overtook the market, Major Angas always calmed him down.

Angas never actually advertised himself a contrarian, but he evidently became one. In the August 1941 letter that announced suspension of the Contrary Opinion service, Neill noted the one contrary thought to keep in mind when everyone was discussing whether or not to buy stocks. Neill urged contrary thinkers to turn the question around. "The most common discussion appears to hinge on whether or not one should buy," he wrote, "whereas, very few (Major Angas excepted) seem to face the problem of selling." (On another level, both men were passionate anti-Communists. Neill frequently warned credulous Americans that communists were old hands at the theory of contrary opinion.)

Being an oddball was one thing. But when the Major let the old hotel become an eyesore filled with papers instead of people, it alarmed Neill, who cultivated a fastidious image. He apologized to friends for inviting Angas to Saxton's River. "I'm so sorry he came," Neill told a friend. "I brought him here, look what he's done to our little town!." The Major lost patience with Neill, the story goes, after asking the Vermont Ruminator what to do with his mountain of papers. Neill advised him to throw it out, which the Major took as an insult. Nevertheless, he remained in Saxton's River until he died painfully in 1972, the victim of a fire started when a kerosene space heater ignited his bathrobe. The Major is buried in Saxton's River, a few feet from his erstwhile friend.

The limelight found Neill again, in 1957, thanks to an obscure dancer with a doctorate in sociology. The dancer, Nicholas Darvas, wrote an overnight sensation, *How I made $2,000,000 in the Stock Market*. Interviewed in *Time* magazine and elsewhere, Darvas credited success to long hours spent studying the market and to wise advice he found in *Tape Reading and Market Tactics*. The widely publicized testimonial propelled Neill's 1931 book into reprints. Never mind the fact that New York's attorney general raised serious questions about whether the mysterious Hungarian hoofer ever really made $2,000,000.

As the Neill Letters of Contrary Opinion approached their tenth anniversary, Neill initiated a more fruitful collaboration with Jim Fraser, a younger disciple of contrary theory. Fraser discovered a kindred spirit. A New York stock broker, he stumbled on Neill's letters while an associate was cleaning out a filing cabinet. Fraser subsequently moved to a town near Albany, New York (not far from Vermont) and called on Neill. They hit it off, and Fraser (once he moved to Vermont, where Neill *insisted* contrarians belong) soon became the publisher of Neill's Letters.

With Fraser's help, Neill also managed to launch the first Contrary Opinion Forum, which has brought contrarians to Vermont every autumn since 1963. One of the speakers was Fidelity Management's Ed Johnson, who spoke on "Contrary Opinion in Stock Market Techniques"—just a few months after Fidelity formed Contrafund, a spiritual offspring of Neill's contrary opinion theory. Contrafund went public in 1967, and Neill bought the first 1,000 shares. Later, in recognition of his guidance, Fidelity paid him a modest retainer in case his advice was needed.

The 1960s produced a stock market desperate for contrary opinions, and Neill obliged. He doubted the widespread expectation that 1960 would supply a magical overture for the rest of the decade. It didn't. The S&P eked out a .4 percent gain. He warned about the mania for stock in every company that sounded like it did anything to do with technology. That crowd took a licking in 1961. By early 1966 the Dow Jones Industrial Average was edging toward the 1000 mark for the first time. Investors were drooling with anticipation. In February, he issued this warning: "It seems clear something must give. A breakaway of some kind appears likely soon.... So we have to be contrary and look at the bear side." As the Sixth Contrary Opinion Forum convened in October, the market was down 250 points from its exuberant start. Neill used the occasion to scold assembled contrarians for being *too bearish*. In 1967, the S&P zoomed up by almost 25 percent.

He decried the performance stocks and their go-go purveyors. Then, as the market hurtled again toward 1000 in late 1968, and experts said for sure it would cross the barrier this time, contrary opinion made Neill a skeptic. "Dear Contrarian," he wrote in December 1968, "Have you ridden a roller coaster lately? They tear around at 75 miles an hour, I'm told. Too scary for me! And so is the 1969 stock market. Just thinking about it gives me the shivers." Those who heeded this warning buffered themselves against a precipitous plunge as the Dow skidded from 985 to 635.

On learning of Neill's plan to retire, Ed Johnson called from Fidelity. Evelyn jotted the message down. "Ed Johnson just called Humphrey from his office in Boston, and told him that his friends at Fidelity when they got the word of Humphrey's decision of stopping Neill letters at the end of 1974 all said how much they would miss it. (Fidelity has 3 or 4 subscriptions.) Ed said the consensus of opinion among them was 'Nobody can put himself into his writing as Humphrey does.'"

The last Neill Letter of Contrary Opinion reached subscribers in December 1974, also the year in which the Great Contrarian attended the October Contrary Opinion Forum for the last time. Having burst many balloons in twenty-five years, he was glad to end on a sanguine note—in contrast to widely held, dark, depressing assessments. His optimism was right on the money. In 1975, the S&P 500 gained more than 54 percent.

As stocks soared, Caxton Printers published The Ruminator, an updated collection of contrary opinion columns written for the *Bellow's Falls Times*. The reviewer for the Financial Analysts Journal offered apt praise. "All in all, Humphrey Neill has scored again with a concise book that contains a wealth of real down-to-earth Vermont 'horse sense' and a bountiful basket of 'common sense.'" A fitting epitaph, indeed, for the Great Contrarian of Saxton's River, Vermont.

Index

About the Author

JOURNALIST STEVEN L. MINTZ HAS COVERED BUSINESS AND finance since 1981. A former Senior Writer at *Corporate Finance Magazine*, Finance Editor at the *American Banker* newspaper and a contributor to *Institutional Investor* and *Financial World*, he is currently the New York Bureau Chief at *CFO Magazine*, a publication of the Economist Group. He and his wife, Melissa, live in Montclair, New Jersey with their two sons, Ben and Thomas, who already display strong contrarian leanings.